Contemporary Fashion Illustration Techniques

Naoki Watanabe

Contemporary Fashion Illustration Techniques
by Naoki Watanabe

First designed and published in Japan in 2008
by Graphic-sha Publishing Co., Ltd.
1-14-17 Kudan-kita, Chiyoda-ku,
Tokyo 102-0073 Japan

English edition published in 2009
by Rockport Publishers, Inc.

First published in the United States of America by
Rockport Publishers, a member of
Quayside Publishing Group
100 Cummings Center
Suite 406-L
Beverly, Massachusetts 01915-6101
Telephone: (978) 282-9590
Fax: (978) 282-2742
www.rockpub.com

ISBN-13: 978-1-59253-556-9
ISBN-10: 1-59253-556-9

10 9 8 7 6 5 4 3 2

Original design: Noboru Okano
Cover image: Naoki Watanabe
Photography: Sotaro Hirose
Model: Miki Kobayashi (swanky)
Cooperation: Junko Yamamoto (Kuwasawa Design School)

English edition layout: Shinichi Ishioka
English translation: Hedges Design Plus
Japanese edition editor: Sachiko Oba (Graphic-sha Publishing Co., Ltd.)
Foreign project management: Kumiko Sakamoto (Graphic-sha Publishing Co., Ltd.)

Printed and bound in China

Introduction

It is by making drawings and experimenting with images on paper that fashion designers develop and give shape to their creative ideas. What is contained in this book is information about fashion design drawing—a vital element that serves as the starting point of garment creation.

For students, studying the foundation of fashion and means of expression, and for anyone involved in apparel design, the act of drawing is at times enjoyable and at other times arduous. With the joy of drawing, there concurrently exist various constraints in a garment's conceptual drawing. For example, even when you are capable of making an attractive and skillful fashion design drawing, no garment will result from it unless there is a strong desire for it to be made. Rather than drawing with superficial skill, focus with serious commitment, and from that drawing a garment will be made. As a result, your commitment will manifest itself in various ways on that piece of paper. On some days you will find it easy to draw, and on others you will not be able to draw at all. But the more experience you have, the sooner your drawings will be able to express your own unique designs. Numerous amendments and changes are made before a final style is achieved. Therefore, it is essential for designers to make many representations of a garment at its conceptual drawing stage.

The impact and quality derived from a garment differs between one created by gathering photographs and information and unstitching sample garments, and one created by a single design drawing made with great care. I would like students to be aware of this point and for professionals working in the field to once again reconfirm it.

In this book I will provide explanation and interweave new interpretations, so that you will be able to master the basics of fashion design drawing—this includes technical drawing as well as color illustrations. I assure you that you can find a drawing that only you can draw and I encourage you to place high value on this.

CONTENTS

Lesson 3 Coloring Technique

Lesson 4 Exercise by Garment Item

Lesson **1** **The Basics of Fashion Design Drawing**

1 Body Proportion

Understanding the Beauty of the Body

The human body is beautiful and attractive like a work of art. Observe its form, before designing with a fabric. Grasping the body image will assure the creation of good design.

In Lesson 1, we will draw the body and its movements repeatedly to master the basics of fashion design drawing.

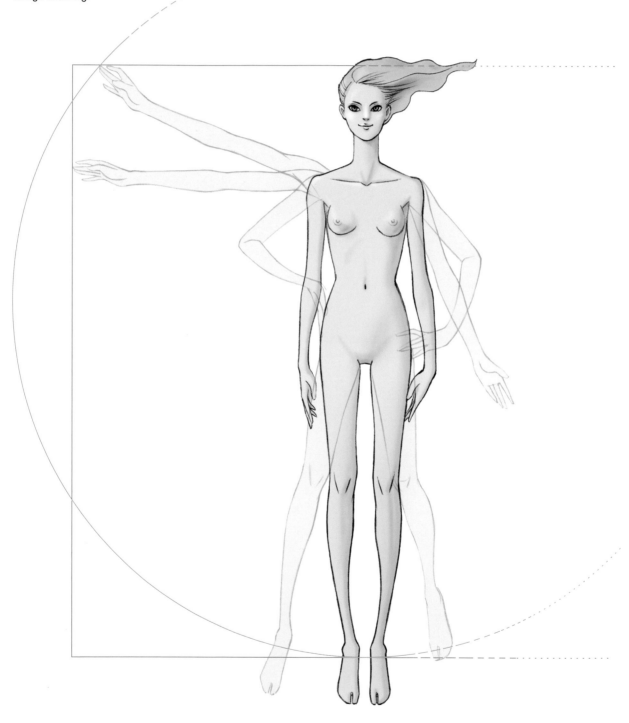

Bone Structure/Joints

The bone structure comprising the base of the human body consists entirely of curved lines. We can move these curved bones freely using the joints and muscles. Although the proportion of the bone structure changes during the course of growth regardless of gender, the position and number of joints remain the same. The yellow parts in the illustrations below represent the flexibly bendable vertebra and 12 main joints. The small joints of the face, hands and feet are not shown here, and please note and learn that the areas of these larger joints are not consistent in terms of their form.

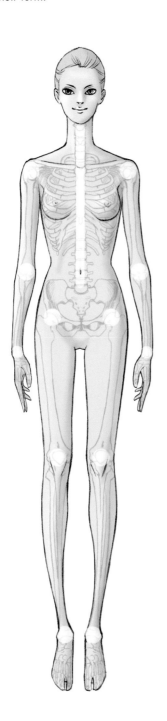

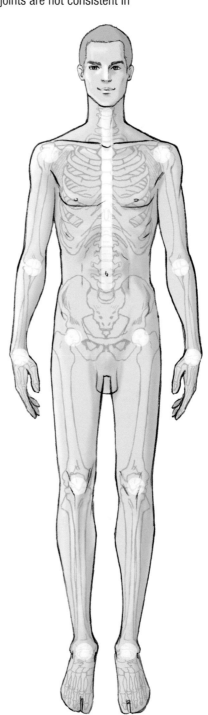

Drawing in 8-Head Proportion

No human body has a beautiful proportion like the one shown below. However in order to depict the human body on a flat surface such as paper, it is necessary to set a visual balance. Here, the drawing is based on the so-called ideal 8-head proportion.

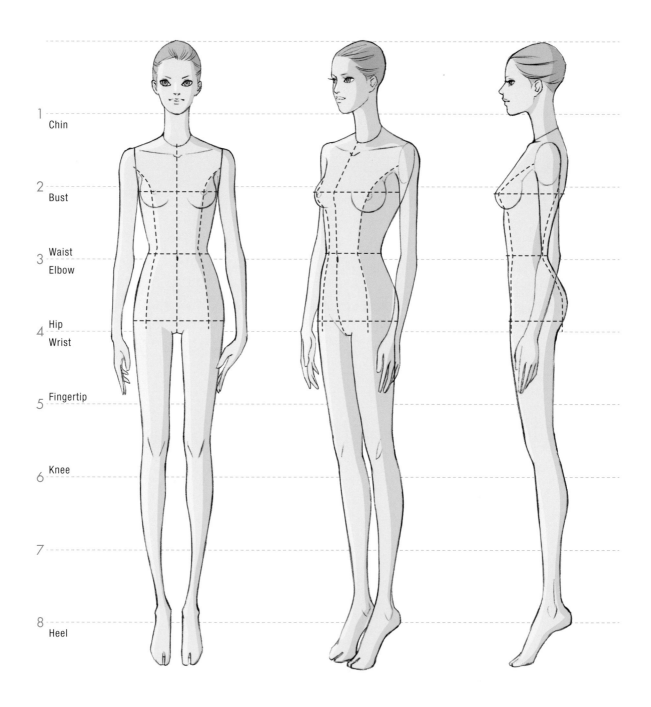

1 Chin

2 Bust

3 Waist
Elbow

4 Hip
Wrist

5 Fingertip

6 Knee

7

8 Heel

In adults, the body, although it varies between individuals, has more or less the same proportion. It is common that the bustline comes at the 2-head position, the elbow and waistline at the 3-head position, hipline at the 4-head position, and the fingertips at the 5-head position respectively. Later we will also use the 7.5-head, 8.5-head, and at times overdraw in the 9-head or 10-head proportion, but first be sure to master the 8-head proportion.

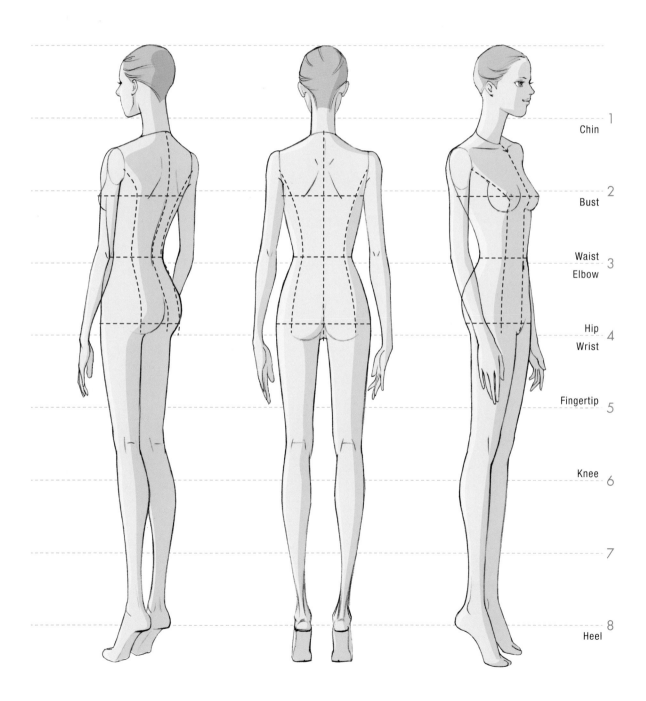

Chin	1
Bust	2
Waist / Elbow	3
Hip / Wrist	4
Fingertip	5
Knee	6
	7
Heel	8

Understanding Position and Width

The following five figures are all based on the 8-head proportion, but with a different width and/or position of the shoulders, waist and hips. Figures A and B are the easiest ones with which to obtain a good balance when dressed. On the other hand, a garment on figures C, D and E will not represent the design that you intend.

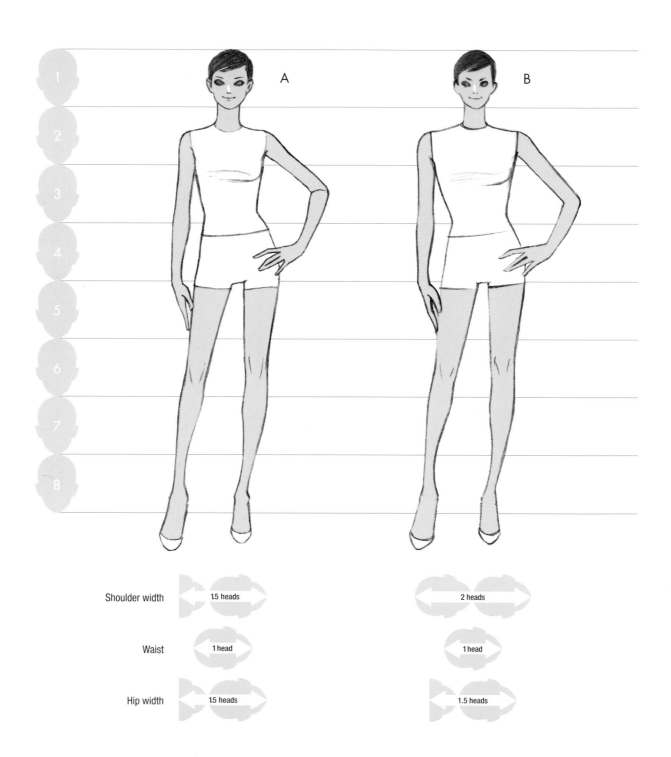

Shoulder width	1.5 heads	2 heads
Waist	1 head	1 head
Hip width	1.5 heads	1.5 heads

Be sure to remember that the garment will look totally different on the wrong body proportion. Even when starting with the 8-head proportion, you may easily end up drawing out of proportion without realizing it. To avoid this, keep the following measurement guide in mind; shoulder width 1.5 head-length, waist 1 head-length and hip 1.5 head-length.

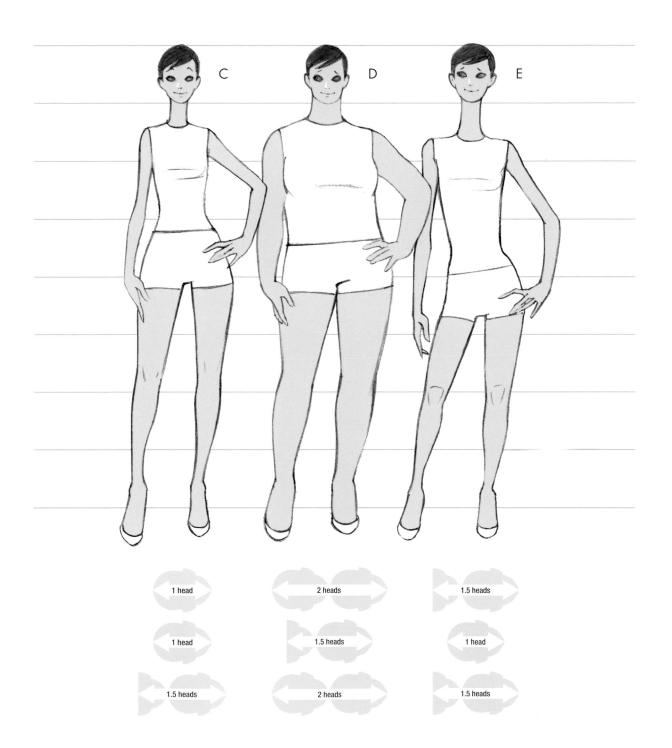

A Useful Measurement Method

There are some simple rules concerning the proportions of the body parts, such as hands, arms, feet, legs and torso. Once you remember them, they will be very helpful in making design drawings.

Use the head-length units cleverly, and you can easily be assured of the right balance, when drawing various poses as shown on the right hand page.

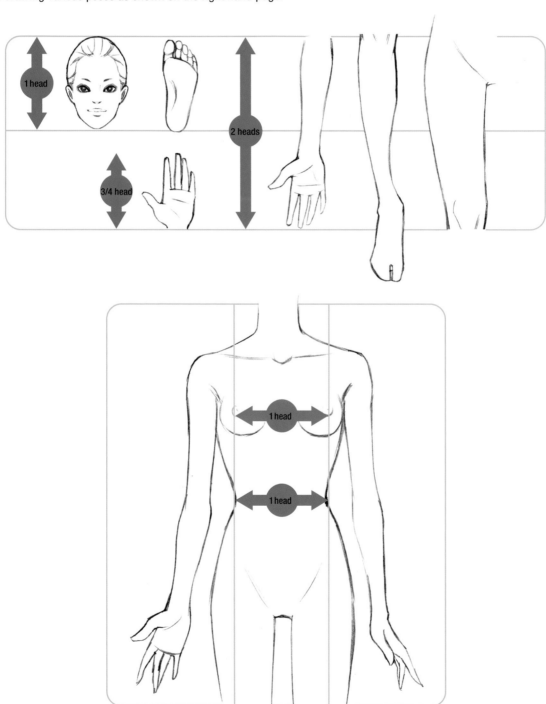

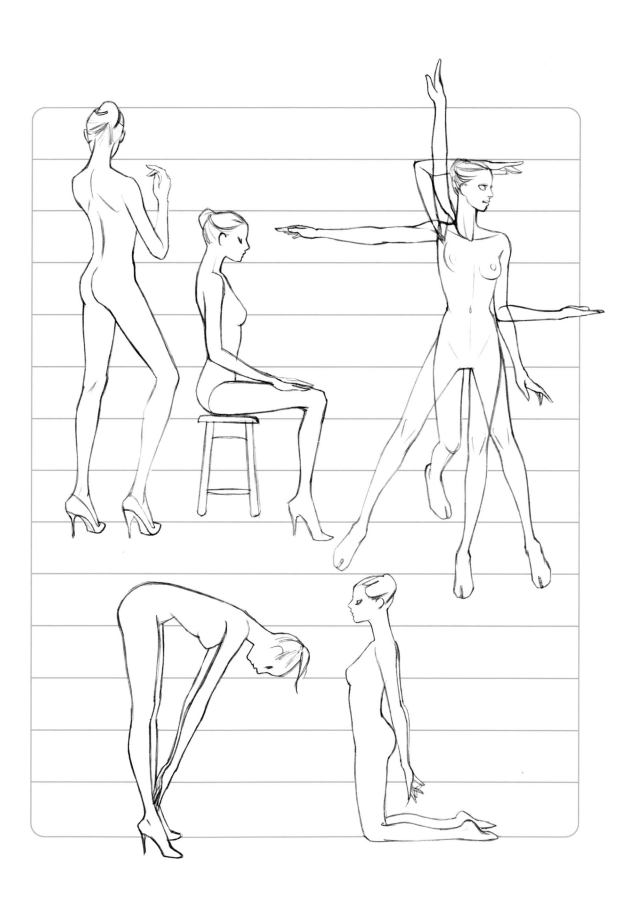

2 Drawing the Head

Face (Front)

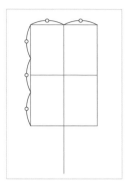

1.
Draw a frame to a ratio of 2 (W) x 3 (H), e.g. 3.2in x 4.8in (8cm x 12cm) or 2.4in x 3.6 in (6cm x 9cm), and divide in half vertically and horizontally.

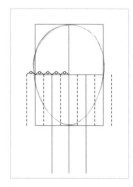

2.
Draw an inverted egg, with the sides of the upper part extending slightly beyond the frame. Don't make the chin too pointed.

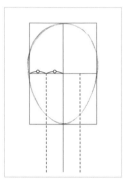

3.
Halve the spaces on both sides of the vertical centerline by drawing lines.

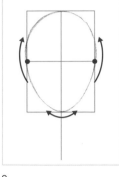

4.
Halve the spaces again, and add lines with equal intervals outside the frame.

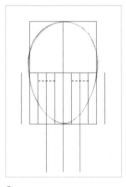

5.
Draw horizontal lines of equal length at the lower eyelids.

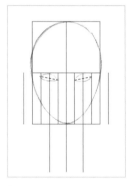

6.
Draw an outline of the eyes, making the outer corners a little higher.

7.
Draw the irises extending over the upper and lower eyelid lines.

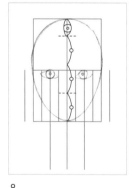

8.
Make a mark on the centerline 1 eye width below top of head. Divide the rest into 3. Position bottom of nose 1/3 above chin.

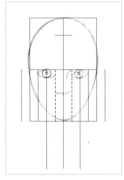

9.
Draw bottom of nose narrower than space between the eyes, and the nose as a single line from either side of inner corners of the eyes.

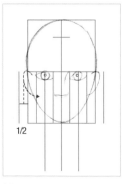

10.
Draw ears starting from a point near the corners of the eyes in a curve toward tip of nose, making them the same length as the nose.

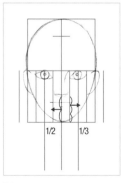

11.
Position bottom of lower lip and center of lips as above. Draw lips slightly wider than space between the eyes.

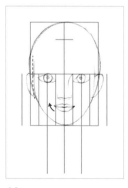

12.
Draw the lips. The corner angle determines facial expression. Modify the outline of the face inward from below the nose.

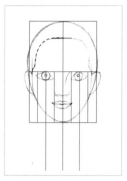

13.
Draw the hairline starting
from the mark made in 8,
in a gentle curve toward the
outer corner of the eye down
to the ear.

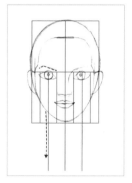

14.
Draw eyebrows starting from
above inner corner of the
eye upward 2/3 and then
downward toward top of the
ear. Add the neckline.

15.
Draw the flow of hair, and
add eyeshadow.

Face (Profile)

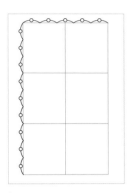

1.
Draw a frame to a ratio of 5 (W) x 9 (H), e.g. 4in x 7.2in (10cm x 18cm), and divide in 3 vertically and in half horizontally.

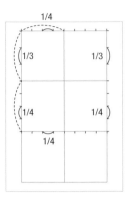

2.
Mark divisions for guidelines as above.

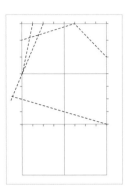

3.
Draw lightly 5 guidelines as above.

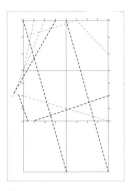

4.
Draw 5 more.

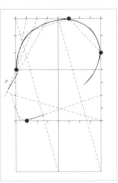

5.
Draw the lines of the skull, nose and chin.

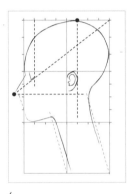

6.
Mark position of lower eyelid with a 'V' based on the guideline. Draw the ear based on the top of head and nose. Make the neck a little narrow.

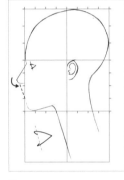

7.
Draw the top and bottom parts of the nose. Make tip of nose a little curved. Draw upper and lower eyelids.

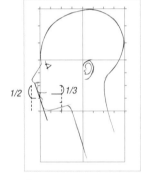

8.
Draw the mouth based on the guideline from bottom of nose to chin. Position the mouth and lower lip as above.

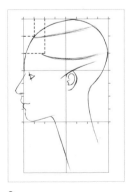

9.
Draw the flow of hair, establishing the hairline position.

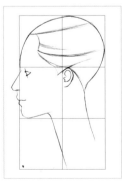

10.
Complete the hairline.

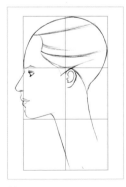

11.
Draw the eyebrow and complete the eyelids and lips.

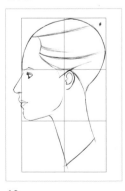

12.
Draw the jawline below the ear, and add the base line of the neck.

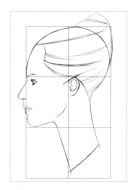

13.
Draw the iris of the eye. Add hairlines to complete the chignon.

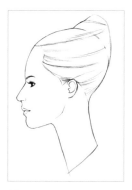

14.
Add eyeshadow.

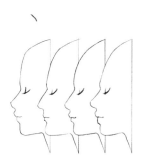

Varying profile lines even a little can influence facial expression greatly. Practice your favorite one.

Face (Diagonal)

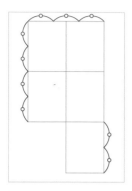

1.
Draw a frame to a ratio of 3 (W) x 4 (H), e.g. 3.6in x 4.8in (9cm x 12cm). Divide in half vertically and horizontally. Add another unit at bottom right.

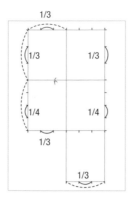

2.
Mark divisions for guidelines as above.

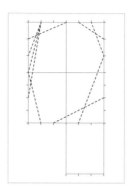

3.
Draw lightly 9 guidelines as above.

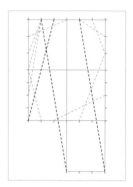

4.
Draw 3 more.

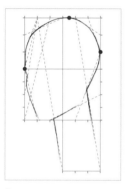

5.
Draw the outline of the head and neck.

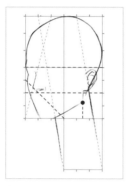

6.
Draw the nose and ear by adding guidelines. Draw the jawline below the ear.

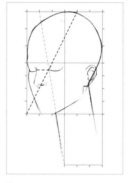

7.
Add a guideline as above to obtain the position of the inner corner of the eye. Draw the lower eyelid as a curve.

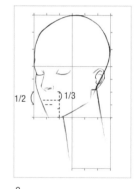

8.
Position the mouth and lower lip as above.

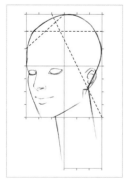

9.
Lightly draw the mouth and lower lip line. Establish the hairline by adding guidelines.

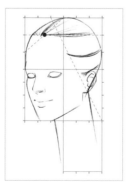

10.
Draw the flow of hair running towards the back of the head.

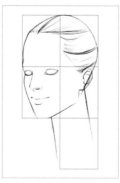

11.
Complete the hairline.

12.
Draw the eyebrow and complete the eyelids and lips.

13.
Draw the jawline as a curve.

14.
Add the irises, and complete
the eyebrows and chignon.

15.
Complete the eyes by adding
make-up.

Eyes/Eyebrows

Eyes

The eyes can play an important role in fashion design drawings. For example, their form greatly influences the model's impression. Practice well so that you can portray a model whose expression is suitable for the design of the garment.

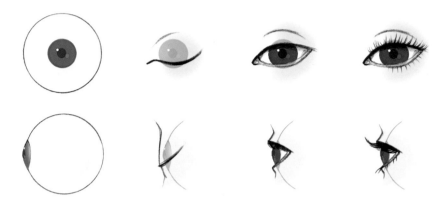

The eye consists of an eyeball and eyelids. The thickness of the eyelid creates a shadow. You can draw eyes with a natural and gentle look by overlaying eyelashes on the shadow.

First draw a guideline joining the inner and outer corners, and draw the upper and lower eyelids as a curve. Continue by drawing the thickness of the eyelids, making the irises partially hidden behind them. Draw the upper eyelashes from the back of the eyelid, and the lower ones from the front edge.

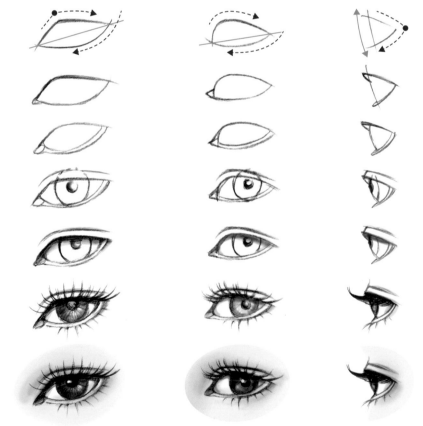

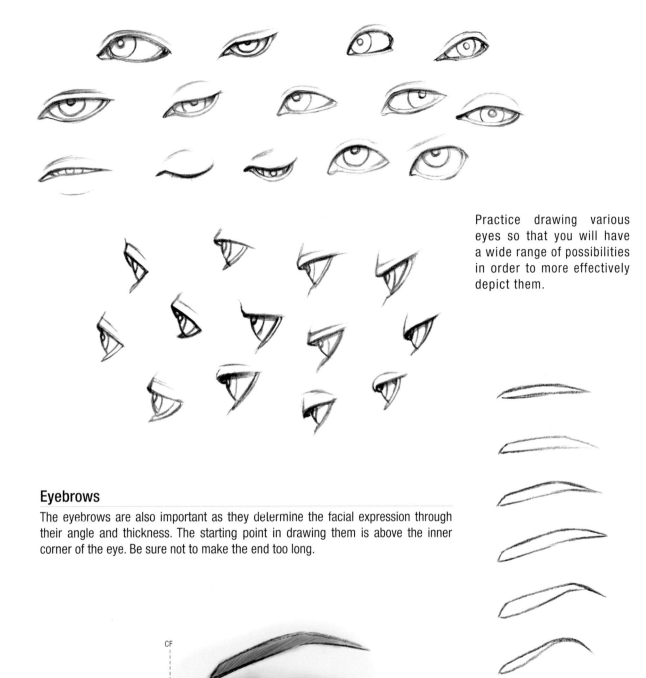

Practice drawing various eyes so that you will have a wide range of possibilities in order to more effectively depict them.

Eyebrows

The eyebrows are also important as they determine the facial expression through their angle and thickness. The starting point in drawing them is above the inner corner of the eye. Be sure not to make the end too long.

CF

Nose/Ears/Lips

Nose

In fashion design drawings, the nose is always simplified. Draw the minimum without going into detail. Draw one side of the nose only, and not at the center of the face. Be sure not to represent the nostril as a circle.

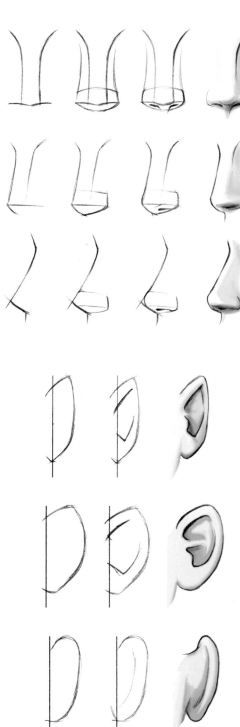

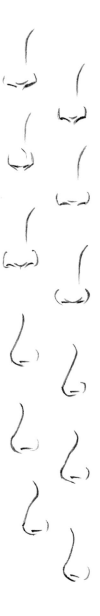

Ears

The ears may be drawn in relation to earrings, spectacles or caps/hats, but similar to the nose, precise details are not necessary. Remember to confirm their position and size, and not to forget to draw the earlobes.

Lips

With their soft and changeable nature, the lips are the key element in expressing the emotion of the model, despite their relatively small size in the drawing. Practice drawing them in your favorite shape.

The upper lip is slightly wider and protrudes a little.

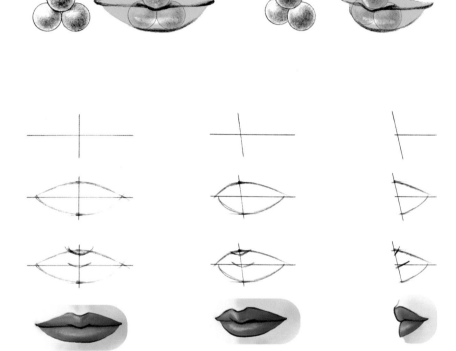

First establish the width and thickness of the lips by drawing their outline as a curve. Then represent the dimple above the upper lip by making the lip's center protrude. Draw the lower lip slightly lighter as it faces upward a little and reflects light.

When the teeth show, be sure not to make them too obvious. Remember also that the face of the model is the minor part in fashion design drawings. Overdrawing it will only hinder in communicating the intended garment design.

Hair Volume and Flow

Hair

The hairstyle, together with make-up, is a very important element which determines the image of the entire style. Pay special attention to its balance.

As a basic exercise, first practice with a tied back style in which the hair is flat on the head. Be sure to allow a little distance between the skull and hair. Draw the flow of hair in quick curving strokes from the hairline to the tie, without bordering the face and hairline. Draw in several synchronized lines for a natural look. Then gradually advance to various hairstyles by increasing the volume of the hair, but note that the distance between the skull and hair is not consistent.

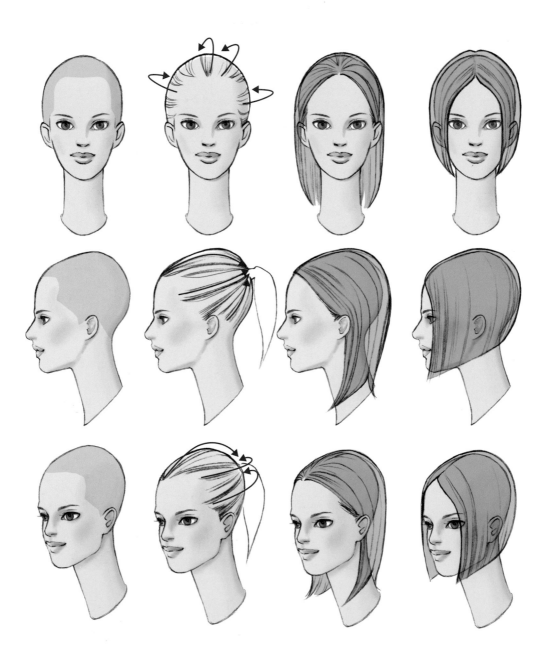

Develop applications by mastering
the flow and movement of hair.

Hats/Caps

Hats

With many different origins and histories, hats come in various types and have many uses. They have as great an impact on fashion design as hairstyle and make-up.

Hats usually consist of the crown which covers the head and the brim. First draw the rim around the head, and then the outer circumference of the brim. Finally, combine the crown and brim while paying attention to the top and underside of the brim.

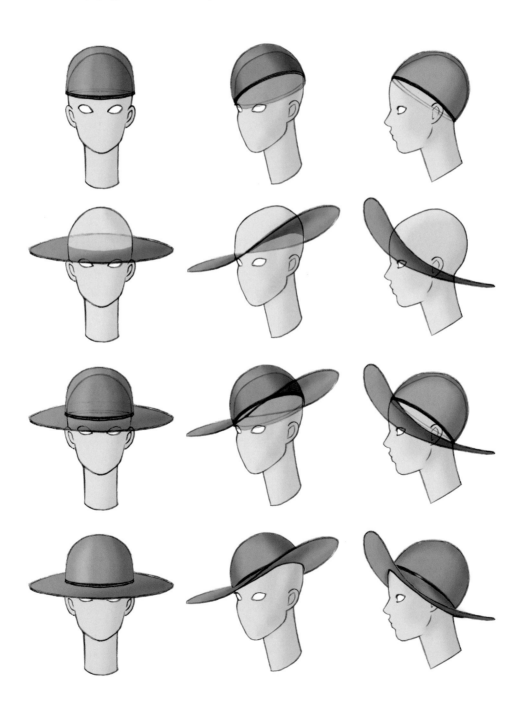

Headgear with its dominant appearance comes in a wide range of styles, from a simple one to those which look different depending on their brim angles. Make it a habit to observe them carefully so that you understand the relation between the crown and brim.

3 Drawing Arms and Legs

Arms/Hands

Arms

The arms, serving as the core of sleeves, play a key role in accentuating the model's pose. Being at the sides of the body, they relate to the sideline and silhouette of the garment in fashion design drawings. Note that they should never interfere with good rendition of such garment design elements, no matter how well the arms themselves are drawn. Focus on how they can compliment the sleeves and garment.

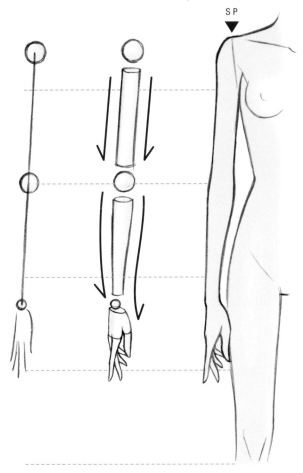

The arm begins at the shoulder point (SP) with the elbow at the waist, the wrist at the crotch and the fingertip at about half way between the knee and hip. The upper arm is straight like a pipe except for the deltoid muscle at the shoulder. The lower arm outlines extend as slight curves, with the inner outline forming a narrow 'S' towards the thumb.

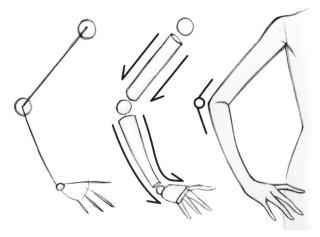

When the arm is bent, the elbow joint forms an acute angle.

Imagine the arm and hand always together. Practice drawing a
curve from the shoulder to the elbow and fingertip in one line.

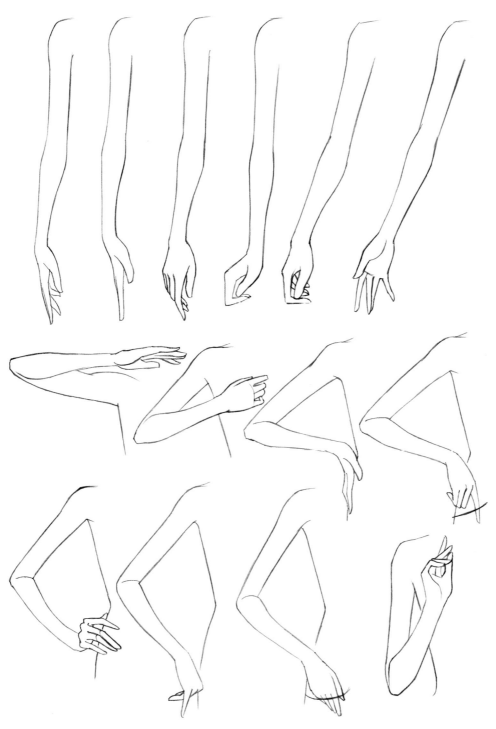

Unless to direct attention to a pocket, the hand on the hip should
be positioned so that the base of the fingers makes contact with
the body outline. Be sure not to draw it too far from the body.

Hands

The length of the hand is three quarters that of the head, and the palm is as long as the middle finger. Observe the base and tips of the fingers, and you will see that they spread like a fan. Draw a bent finger by separating it at each joint.

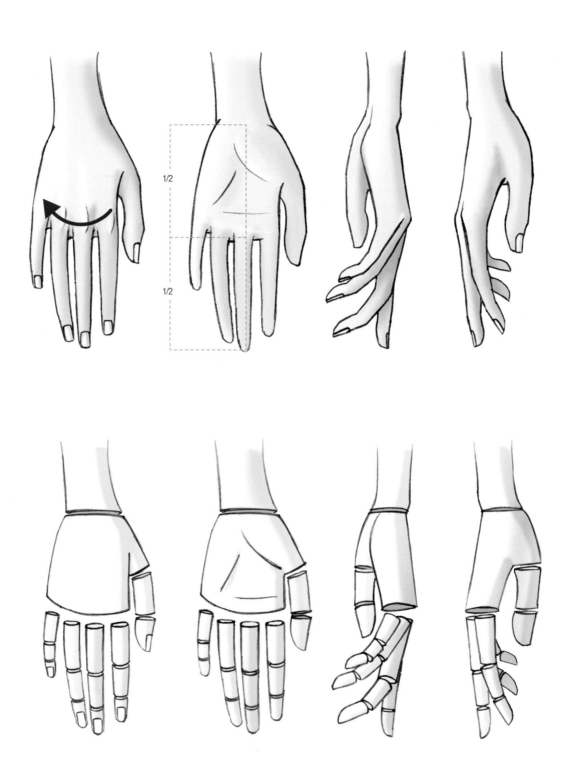

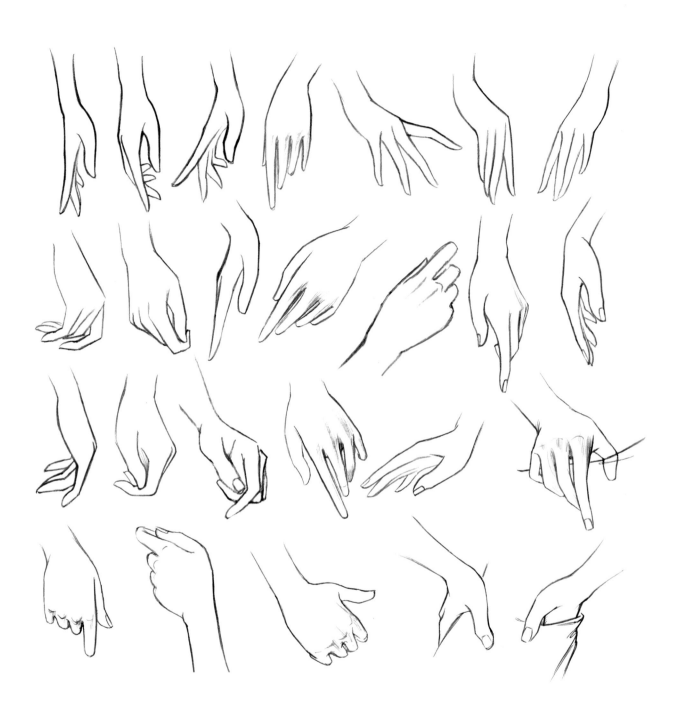

The hand has many different expressions. When applying its complex form to a drawing, master some patterns first, and you can then focus on the design of the garment.

Legs/Feet/Shoes

Being nearly half the body height and supporting the entire body, the legs consist of dynamic elements, compared with the arms. Draw them using dynamic lines with this in mind, and it will help you grasp the image. Although they are often hidden under a garment, you should not neglect practicing to draw them as there are many garments designed to reveal the legs.

Legs

The legs are tilted and do not fall straight down based on the joints. From the frontal view, the outline is similar to that of the arms, except that the dents at the inner and outer sides of the knee differ in position, as do the bones at the ankle joint. When observed from the side, the core muscle lines clearly form an 'S' with a sharply curved end below the calf.

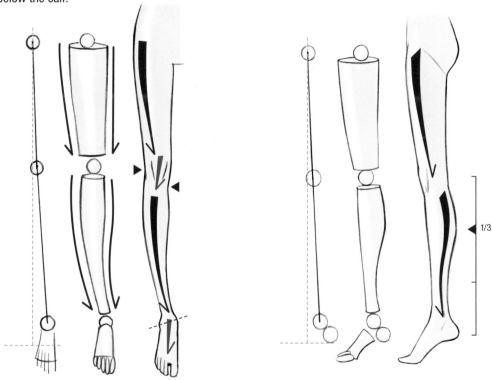

Feet

The foot appears very different depending on the height of the heel, but we hardly draw bare feet in fashion design drawings. Even with sandals, the feet are not completely revealed, and are drawn together with the sole. Master the drawing of feet in different heights of shoe heel.

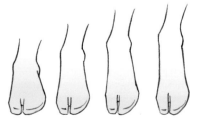
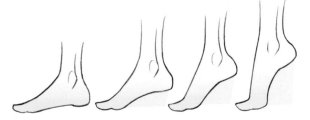

Shoes

Shoes are also one of the key elements in fashion. First grasp the form of the soles of various kinds of footwear, e.g. sandals to boots.

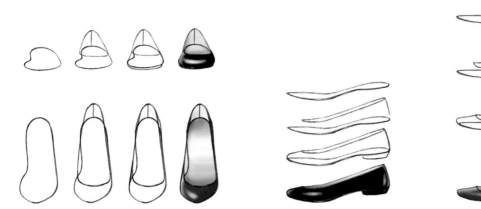

Divide a sole in half vertically and draw the inner line. Decide the height of the heel or sole, and design of the instep. Using precise curves, produce lines as if fitting the shoes to the feet. Be sure to sketch real footwear at least once.

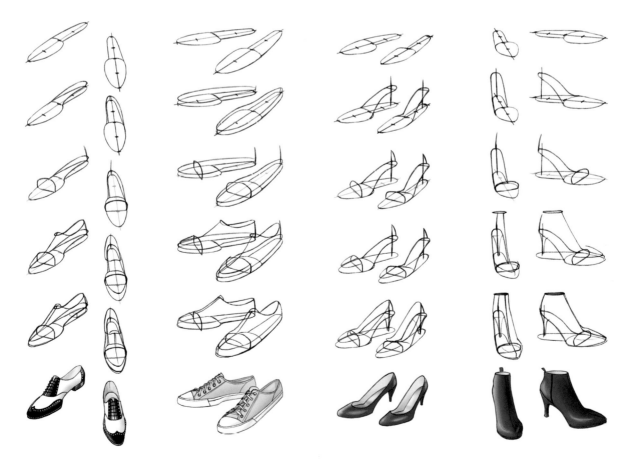

4 Poses

Studying Poses

You can create poses by tilting the bones. In the erect posture, the shoulder tilts together with the vertebrae. Likewise, the pelvis tilts as the weight is shifted to one leg. "When the left shoulder is lowered, the same left hip is raised" — this is the basic rule for various poses.

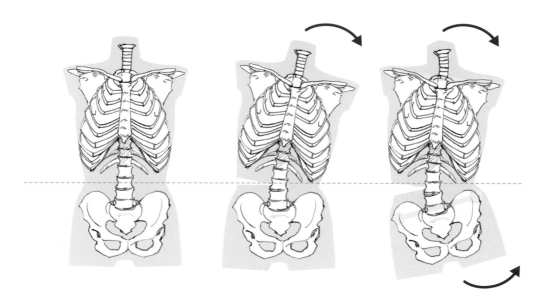

When studying poses, imagine the letter 'H' on its side. As shown in A below, the pose with tilted shoulder and hip, and weight shifted to one leg looks natural, but note that over-tilting will create excessive creases on the garment and a complex composition. Depending on the body movement, the shoulder and hip width-lines can be parallel as shown in B, but be sure not to use such a pose unless it looks natural.

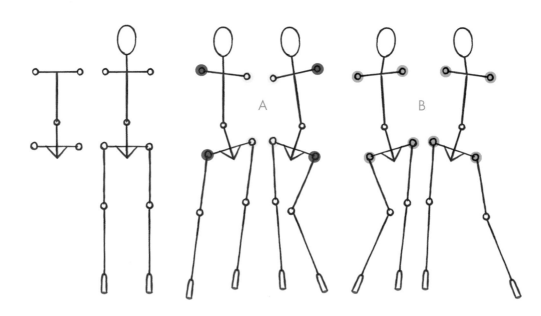

The human frame is more or less symmetrical and its size remains the same in any pose. Poses with both feet on the ground have the same degree of tilting angle in the hips, knees and heels.

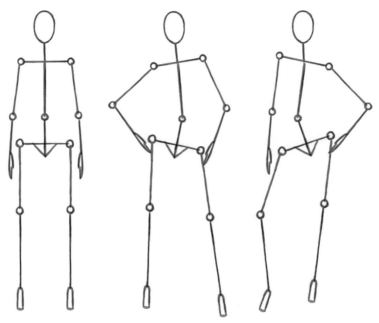

The nude figure A below is in the erect pose, and figure B is the pose with weight on one leg. Figure A differs from B in its tilting angle of the shoulder and hip. Figures C and D appear different again from A and B, but the shape of the torso is nearly the same as B. With the same torso, you can create many poses while dressing different garments, if you master the drawing of various flexible arm and leg movements.

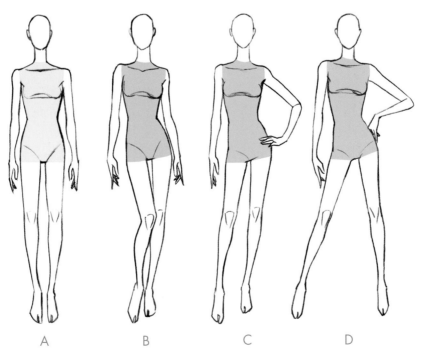

A   B   C   D

Erect Pose

Being symmetrical, the erect pose is the easiest one on which to dress a garment. You do not need to draw unnecessary creases. Practice drawing this basic pose by first calculating the key positions using a ruler, and then complete with curved lines freehand. Repeat this freehand drawing until your hand 'remembers' the rhythm.

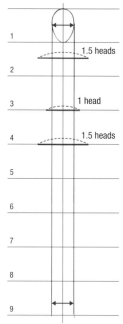

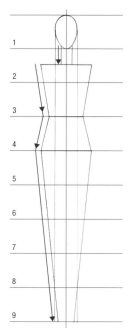

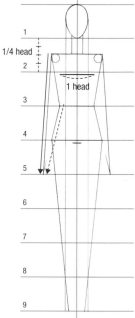

1. Allowing space for hair, divide the centerline into 9 and draw the head in a ratio of 2 (W):3 (H). Draw lines straight down from each side of the head. Draw lines; 1.5, 1 and 1.5 head-widths as above.

2. Draw the neck (1/2 head-width), and guidelines by joining shoulder, waist, and hip. Extend them to Line 9 through the crossing point of the head-width line and Line 8.

3. Draw armlines from shoulder to fingertip position obtained by extending the hipline. Mark ends of shoulders with circles (1/4 head-length). Mark bust top (1 head-length) just below Line 2 and crotch just below Line 4.

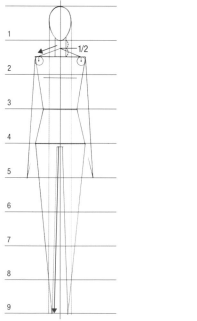

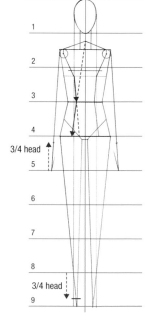

4. Draw shoulderlines from the 1/2 neck height to top of circles. Draw the inner leglines as above.

5. Draw guidelines towards the center of Line 3 from center of the circles to the head-width lines. Draw crotchlines from the 1/2 hipline points to the crotch.

6. Draw lines towards crotch from under the bust to Line 3. Extend to Line 4 as an extension of the dotted line starting from the neck center. Mark the wrist and toe positions (3/4 head-length).

In fashion design drawings, the nude figure is for dressing a garment, and no realistic rendition is necessary. Smooth out the joints and muscles and render them as clean lines. Note also that the nude figure does not remain constant. Adjust the widths of the shoulders, waist and hips according to the current fashion and balance of the garment.

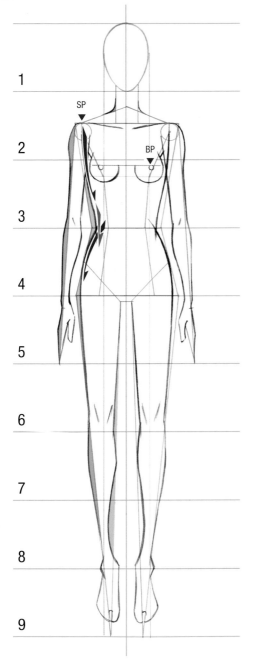

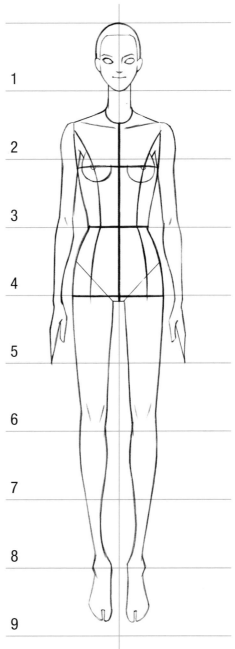

7. Draw muscles and joints by eliminating or adding curves to guidelines. From this stage, draw freehand. Draw a line as a narrow 'S' from SP to the underarm and waist. Draw curved hiplines separately to establish the waist position more easily. Draw the collarbones, breasts and knees.

8. Be sure to draw 6 key structural guidelines for dressing; 3 vertical lines consisting of the centerline, 2 ridgelines dividing the torso into the front and sides, and 3 horizontal lines consisting of the bust, waist, and hip width-lines.

Pose with Weight on One Leg

This pose is used often as it gives movement to fashion design drawings. As it is symmetrical, you can show the line of the side of the body, and at the same time it can easily reveal your fashion sense. Master the pose by repeated practice.

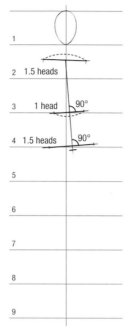

1. Tilt slightly the shoulder, waist, and hip width-lines as shown above. Make the waist and hip width-lines parallel and slightly longer at the higher ends.

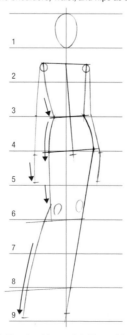

2. Draw a line crossing the waist and hip width-lines at 90° from the center point of the shoulders to the crotch. Mark the widths of the shoulders, waist, and hips as above.

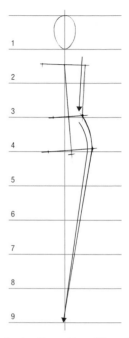

3. Join the shoulder, waist, and hip on the left side and extend the line to the center of Line 9 to represent the outline of the pivotal leg. Give roundness to the hip outline.

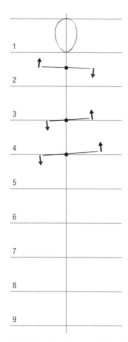

4. Draw guidelines parallel to the hip width-line from the center of Lines 6 and 8.

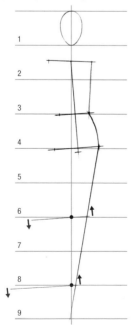

5. Join the shoulder, waist, hip, and knee on the right side. Extend the line to a point just above Line 9, while changing direction. Mark shoulder tips and knees with circles. Draw guidelines for the arms.

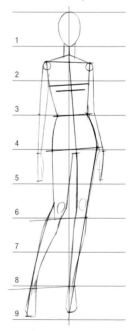

6. Draw the neck, shoulders, arms, inner outline of the legs and feet, as well as the bust and under-bust lines.

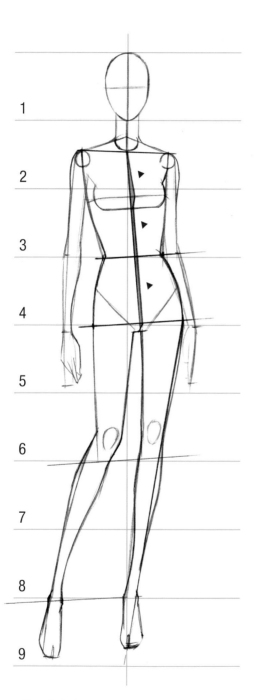

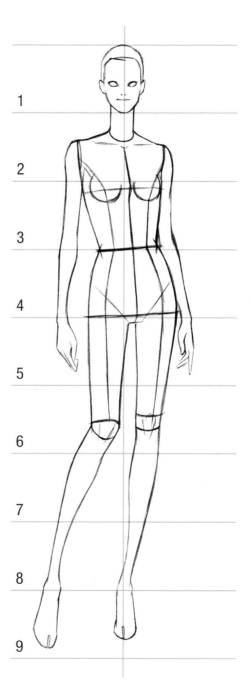

7. Draw the body contours as clean lines. Make the median line appear 3D, by adjusting it, considering the contour from the collarbones to the crotch.

8. Complete the drawing by checking the structural guidelines based on the body angle.

Diagonal Pose (Front Hip Higher)

There are two kinds of diagonal pose with weight on one leg. One is this pose with the front hip higher. It is suitable for the design of garments with a wide hem.

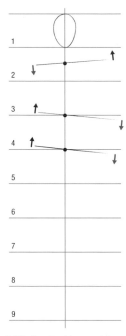

1. Tilt slightly the shoulders, waist, and hips as above. Make the waist and hip width-lines parallel and slightly longer at the higher ends.

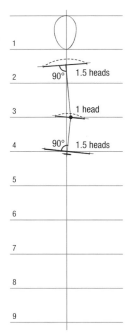

2. Draw a line from the center point of the shoulders to the waist width-line at 90°. Extend it to the crotch at 90° to the hip width-line. Mark the widths of the shoulders, waist, and hips as above.

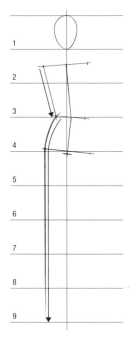

3. Join the shoulder, waist, and hip on the right side and extend vertically as a pivotal leg line to Line 9. Give roundness to the hip outline.

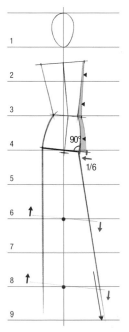

4. Shorten the hip width-line at the lower end by 1/6. Draw the left outline of the torso inward from the shoulder tip and extend it to Line 9 as above. Draw guidelines parallel to the hip width-line as above.

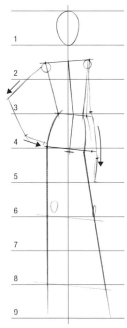

5. Mark the shoulder tips and knees with circles. Draw guidelines for the arms.

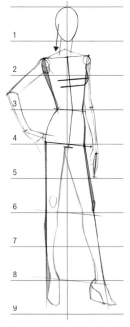

6. Draw the neck slightly tilted, and the shoulders, arms, inner outline of the legs and feet, as well as the bust and under-bust lines.

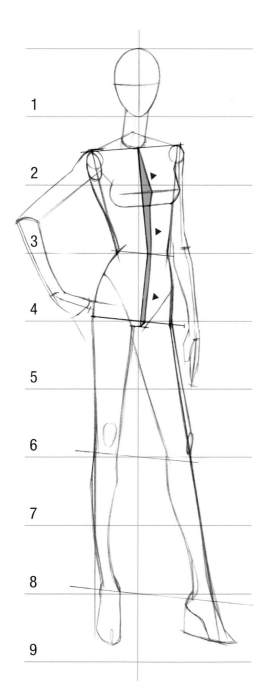

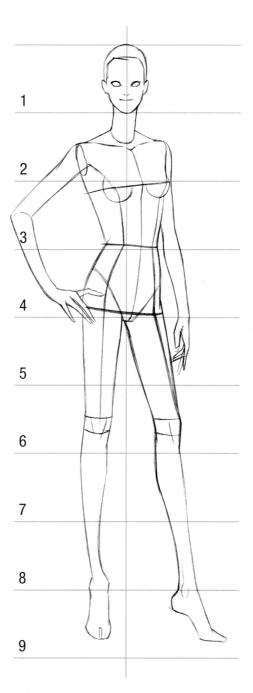

7. Draw the body contours as clean lines. Make the median line appear 3D, by adjusting it, considering the contour from the collarbones to the crotch.

8. Complete the drawing by checking the structural guidelines based on the body angle.

Diagonal Pose (Back Hip Higher)

Another diagonal pose with weight on one leg is this one with the back hip higher.
It can be applied to various designs as it conveys movement easily.

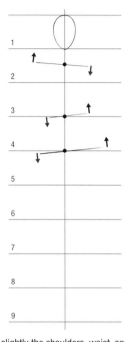

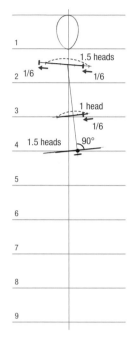

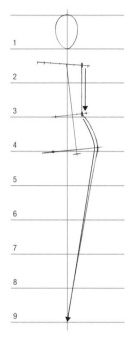

1. Tilt slightly the shoulders, waist, and hips as above. Make the waist and hip width-lines parallel and slightly longer at the higher ends.

2. Draw a line crossing the waist and hip width-lines at 90° from the center point of the shoulders to the crotch. Shift the shoulder by 1/6, and shorten the waste width-line at the higher end by 1/6 as above.

3. Join the shoulder, waist, and hip on the left side and extend the line to the center of Line 9 to represent the outerline of the pivotal leg. Give roundness to the hip outline.

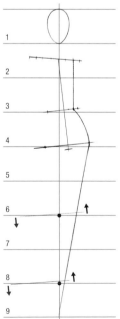

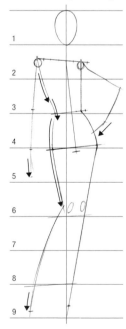

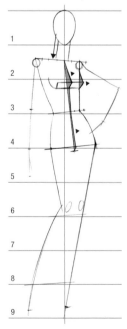

4. Draw guidelines parallel to the hip width-line from the center of Lines 6 and 8.

5. Join the shoulder, waist, hip, and knee on the right side. Extend the line to a point just above Line 9, while changing direction. Mark shoulder tips and knees with circles. Draw guidelines for the arms.

6. Draw the neck slightly tilted. Establish the bust width-line, while shifting toward the back. Draw the median line and back breast line to give a 3D effect.

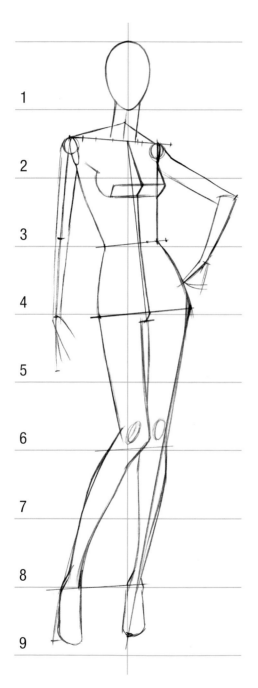

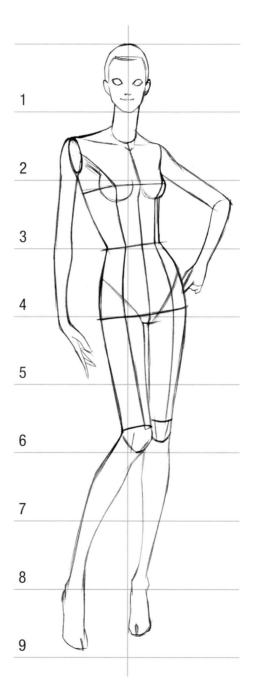

7. Draw the body contours as clean lines.

8. Complete the drawing by checking the structural guidelines based on the body angle.

Pose Variations

With the same torso, you can create an endless variety of poses by controlling the face/head and neck, arms and hands, legs and feet combinations.

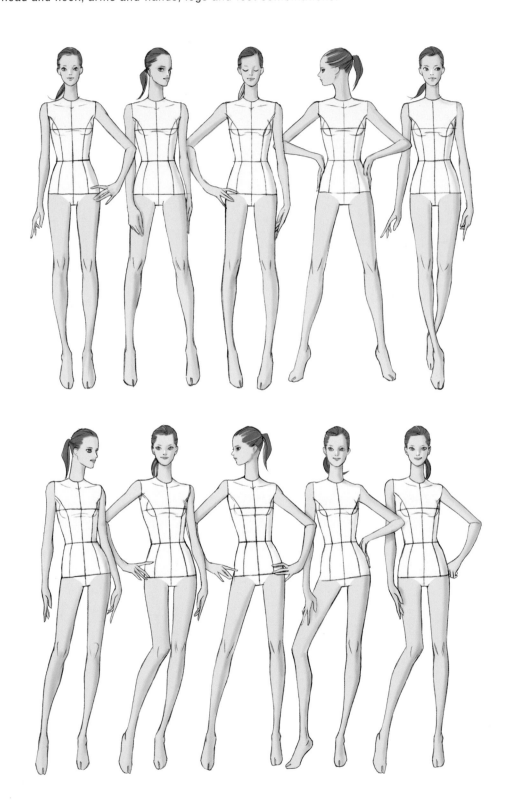

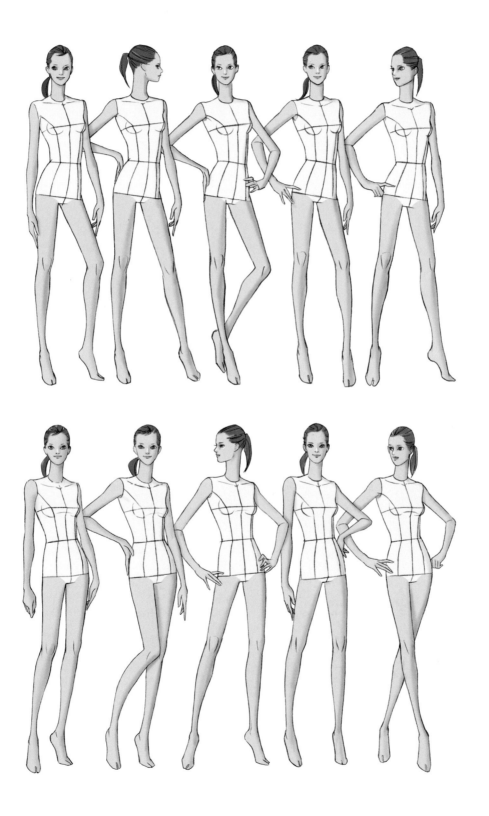

Lesson **2** **Dressing Technique**

1 Dressing

Silhouettes

Dressing means to draw the lines of garments over 'the body' which you learned in Lesson 1, while thoroughly understanding the garment's structure. Be aware that while each line serves as an important element in the final design, it is not necessary for all of them to be realistic. The most important thing is to keep drawing until you achieve the design you desire. By drawing repeatedly, you can simulate and create your own designs.

Unlimited forms are conceivable if you are simply wrapping the body, but in garment design, you can only hang fabric from the shoulders, hips and/or waist with a belt. When representing your ideas as a sketch, be sure to consider which points the fabric is hanging from, and to avoid designs with elements which do not follow gravity or good mobility. In this way, you will find your ideal silhouette.

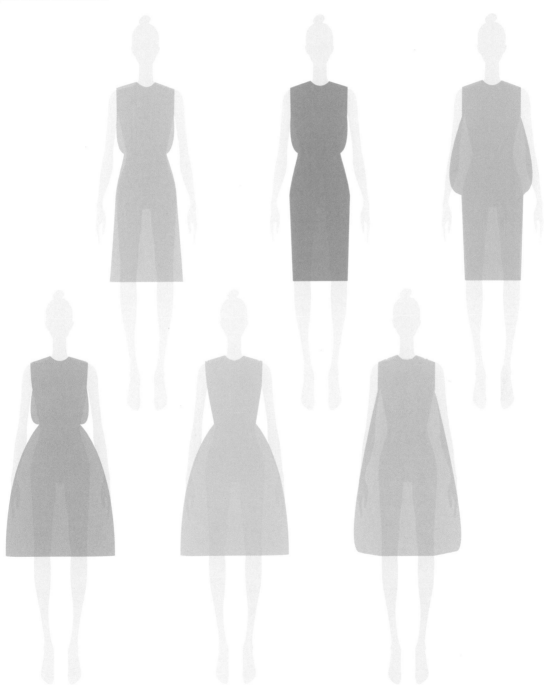

Drawing the Two Dimensional as Three Dimensional

When a three dimensional human body is wrapped by a two dimensional fabric, there will be some space between them. Such spaces, which allow mobility and create beautiful garment lines, depend greatly on the shape and texture of the fabric. In fashion design drawings, dressing involves always having these spaces in mind.

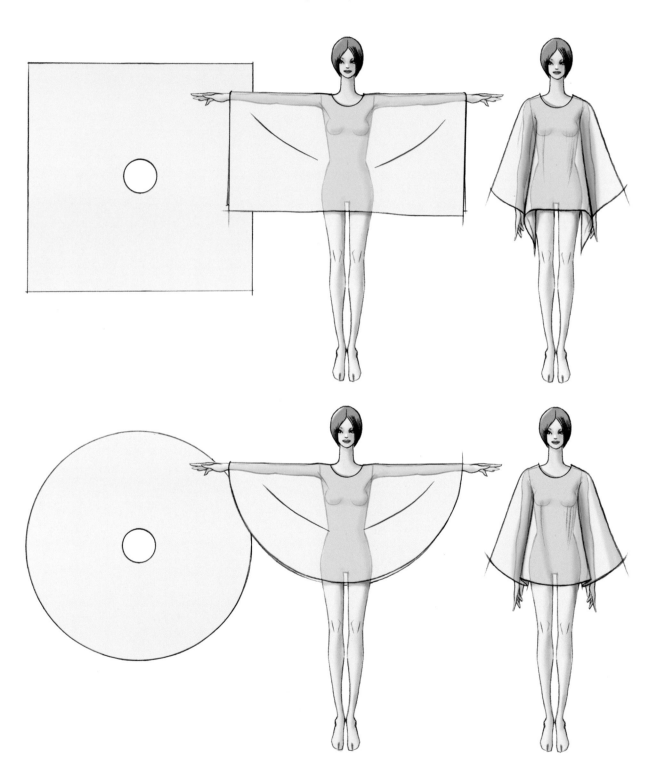

The following illustrations show the body through the garment. It is a basic training in design, not only in fashion, to be able to visualize the underlying form, in order to understand its structure and reconstruct it as a garment. First try to grasp the general structure without worrying about details.

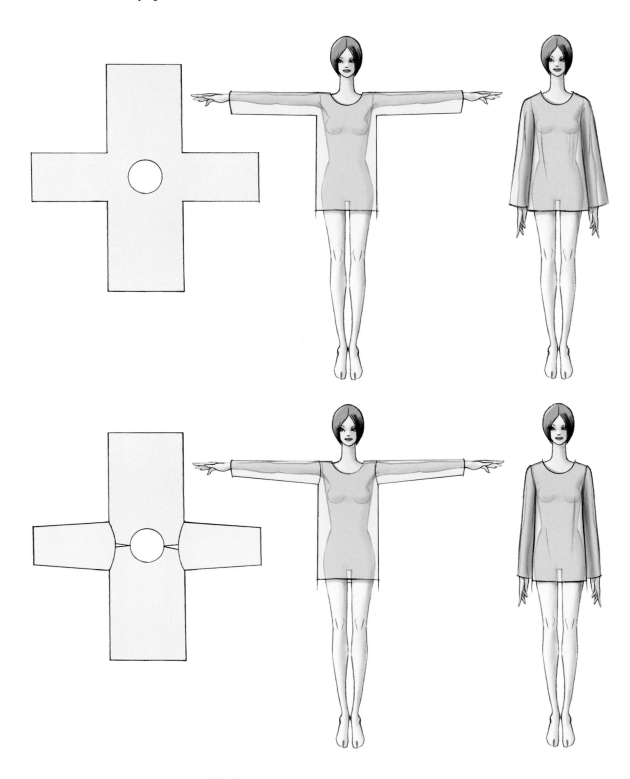

Relation between Fabric and Body

There are spaces between the body and fabric, some are for mobility and others for style. Study which part of the body makes contact with the fabric and which does not, by looking at your own clothing and depicting them in line drawings. Pay extra attention to the arms and legs, while not forgetting to consider gravity.

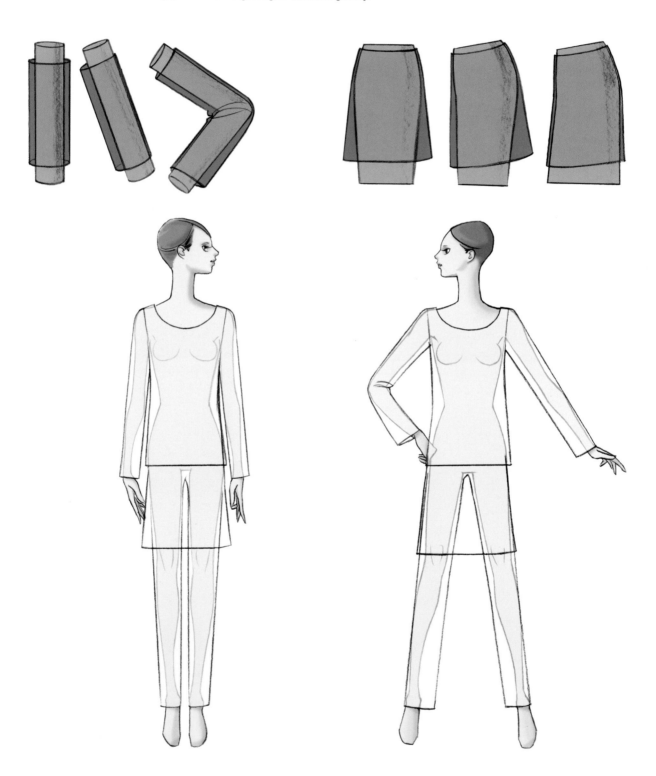

Setting the Viewpoint

Fashion design drawings will be more convincing if the model and garments are portrayed with a certain three dimensional effect. The four models here are seen from various viewpoints. When thinking of the body as a tube, it is clear how important it is to draw the hems correctly.

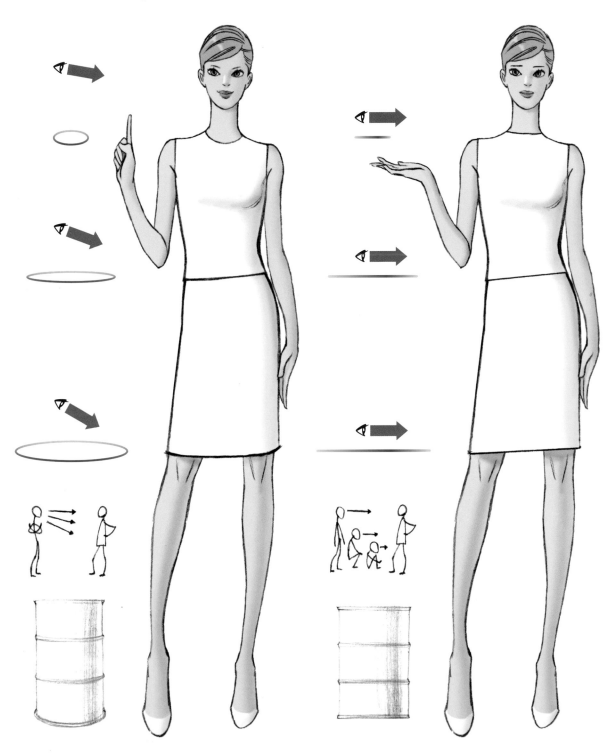

When drawing horizontal lines such as the hem as opposed to vertical lines such as the body sideline, you have to consider its continuing line toward the back. Be sure to set the viewpoint in the right place, so that you can draw your design correctly. The standard viewpoint for fashion design drawings is at the height of the model's eyes and two to three meters away.

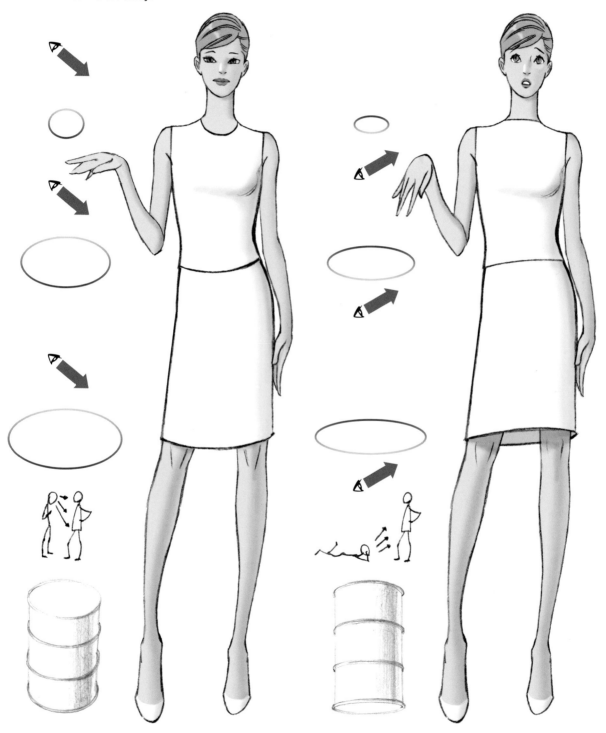

Darts/Gathers/Pleats/Drapes

Darts, gathers, and pleats are used to increase or reduce the garment's volume. These must be considered for structural and functional reasons while making sketches. The rules involve deciding precisely where and in which direction to add or reduce volume.

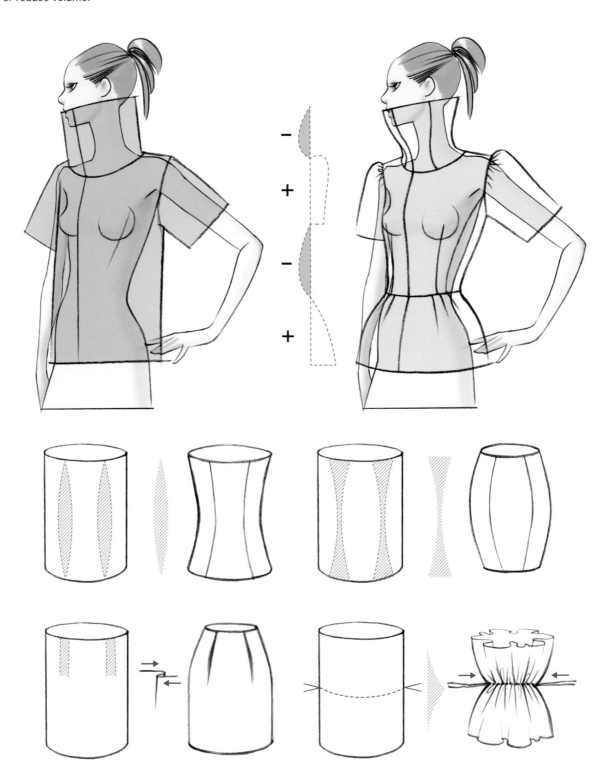

Designers also focus on the volume and direction of drapes which are determined by the direction of the fabric grain, body form, and gravity. Draw drapes by testing how you would like a fabric to look and where to apply them, and so on.

Fabric Characteristics/Creases

While drapes create beautiful lines when stationary, lines created by movement are defined as creases. When the projecting points of a fabric are pulled away from each other, vertical, horizontal, and diagonal creases can appear. All you have to do is to draw soft curves back and forth between these projecting points.

Draw creases starting from the inside of the body, while imagining the texture of the fabric to avoid spoiling the design form. Study the direction of the flow of the fabric.

Use of Various Lines

By varying the thickness of lines, or creating different levels, you can dramatically increase the amount of information conveyed by your design drawing. Adding a little shading along the border line where the fabric is lifted results in a much softer impression.

As shown above, the effects are obvious when adding levels to the side of the waistline.

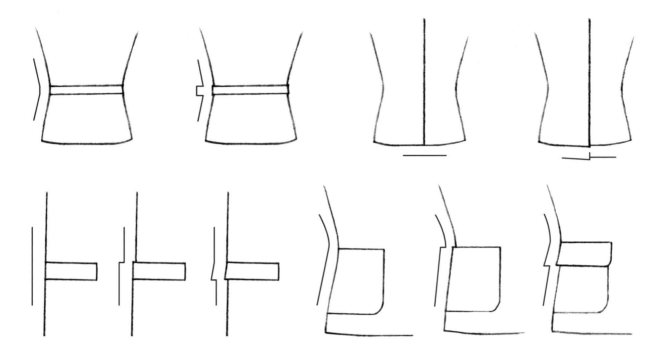

Place importance on the details of your design.

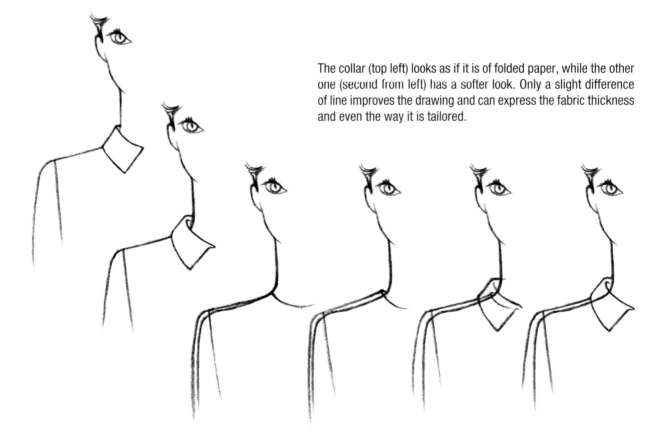

The collar (top left) looks as if it is of folded paper, while the other one (second from left) has a softer look. Only a slight difference of line improves the drawing and can express the fabric thickness and even the way it is tailored.

Sketch

Sketching an actual model within 10 minutes is a very effective way to improve your ability to observe and grasp the bare essentials. As the purpose is to train your eye and develop your hand skill, precision is not necessary. Just concentrate on observing. First, draw the body in loose lines, and gradually advance to the details after grasping the image.

Once you have achieved what you want, after drawing and erasing unwanted lines, you will see that there are hardly any vertical or horizontal lines. Draw people around you whom you find attractive. This is highly recommended as you can try various poses and styles, unlike when drawing professional models.

Drawing from Photographs

The model in the photograph below actually has an eight-head well-proportioned figure, but when we eliminate the shading and color and transfer the outline only, she looks much wider than in the photograph (A). Make the neck, arms, and legs longer, each in the same proportion, and you can portray her and the garments more naturally and beautifully, even without shading and color (B).

A

B

When drawing based on a flat medium such as a photograph, draw in a rather exaggerated way to achieve a better balance on paper. You have no problem finding high quality photographs suitable for practice. Just keep drawing as much as you can.

Lesson **3** **Coloring Technique**

1 Coloring

Drawing Tools and Materials

It is exciting to select drawing tools and materials from the wide variety available. Among all of them the most basic and reliable for fashion design drawing is watercolor. Normally all you need is paper, pencils, and watercolors, but you can optimize the result of your work by combining your favorite tools and materials to ensure quick and consistent quality. The result is what matters, rather than the traditional rules for drawing tools and materials. First use the ones you like based on the various drawing methods introduced on the following pages, and advance to more and different types later.

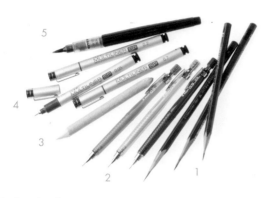

For line drawing:
1. Pencils (3H to 3B)
2. Mechanical pencils
3. Blending stump
4. Drawing pens (Bold/Medium/Fine)
5. Brush pen

For clean/correct work:
1. Rulers and templates
2. Snap-off blade knife
3. Erasers (Normal/kneadable)
4. Paper tape
5. Desk brush
6. Spray fixative

For recording/sketching:
1. Sketch pad
2. Drawing pad
3. Kent paper pad
4. Marker pad
5. Copy paper
6. Tracing paper (Roll)

For greater substance:
Brushes (Thick/Medium/Fine)

For color creation:
1. Paint dish
2. Pallet
3. Brush washer
4. Water dispenser
5. Wiping cloth

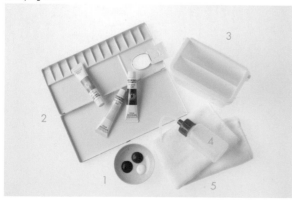

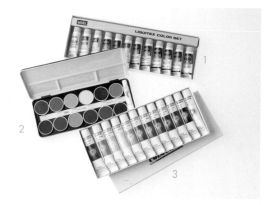

For coloring:
1. Color pencils
2. Markers
3. Pastels

For coloring with brush:
1. Acryl gouache
2. Solid watercolors
3. Watercolors

About Color

First color, then shape and material. Not only in fashion but in all areas of design, color plays a vitally important role. An impression is derived more quickly and strongly from 'color' than from shape. For example when describing an apple in words, we do not give a detailed account of the apple's shape. Just as we might say a 'red apple', when we want to give an impression of something, the color is an essential element. We make drawings in order to explore a design or to communicate it to others, so it is vital to select colors very carefully. Deciding from among the limitless color combinations imaginable is fun, but can also be a headache, and practice in blending them to create a color scheme will certainly help to sharpen your color sense. Remember also that color is constantly advancing. We should always retain an interest in the information produced by international research and the interpretation of color.

In order to precisely understand the color characteristics of a fabric, or to give instructions for printing, you will need to be aware of the 'fundamentals of color', for example the three attributes of hue, brightness, and saturation.

Hue - denotes the characteristic that distinguishes one color from another and allows division into red, orange, yellow, green, blue, purple, etc.

Brightness - denotes the amount of light and shade contained in a color and determines whether it is light or dark and so on.

Saturation - denotes the vividness and strength of colors, from gray and muddy to vivid and pure.

Magenta, yellow, and cyan. These three can be used to make up all other colors. However, they cannot be made by mixing colors and are therefore called primary colors.

Cyan   Magenta   Yellow

Magenta (M) + yellow (Y) = red (R)
Yellow (Y) + cyan (C) = green (G)
Cyan (C) + magenta (M) = blue (B)

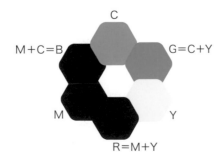

C

M+C=B   G=C+Y

M   Y

R=M+Y

Color gradation can be further controlled using white and black.

White   Black

Mixing Color

Since a design drawing is essentially 'a conceptual drawing of a garment', the choice of colors should be driven by your instinctive feeling. The number of colors you need to use on a design drawing, in other words, the conceptual drawing, is not very great. Likewise, the amount of color used and the area of the drawing to be colored need be only very small. In that case, why not take time and effort in selecting the right colors and creating on the palette the colors you have in mind. Deciding the color and mixing it is more important than the act and method of applying it. Sometimes a color created accidentally on the palette will broaden your choices. Making color is not a matter of calculation but of feeling.

But what is the color we use for design drawings? Naturally, it is the color of fabric. By mixing paints we can make a whole range of colors, but beginners tend to paint with those close to the pure colors that come straight out of the tube. Also, if you spend too long thinking about the next color, you end up choosing it from one of the tubes, and the result is a set of rainbow colors. It is fine to enjoy color, but we may end up forgetting that the color of the fabric should be what matches the color of the skin. The principle that when choosing color we should start by matching it to the skin is an important point in design drawing.

When adjusting color to match the color of the skin, there is a technique of adding a very little white or black. When for instance you have already decided on the fabric to use and you need a design drawing that reproduces its color faithfully, this technique is highly recommended.

Drawings Using Various Tools/Materials

You can use watercolors, markers, color pencils, and pastels for coloring,
and pencils, color pencils, brush-pens, and drawing pens for drawing lines.
The ideal medium is watercolor, but combine others for a better result.

Drawing paper
Markers
Color pencils

Copy paper
Pastels
Color pencils

Drawing paper
Gouache (Opaque watercolors)
Color pencils

Drawing paper
Markers
Color pencils

Kent paper
Markers
Color pencils

Drawing paper
Watercolors
Pencil

Drawing paper
Watercolors
Markers
Color pencils

Drawing paper
Watercolors
Markers
Color pencils

Drawing paper
Markers
Brush-pens

Drawing paper
Watercolors
Pastels

Solid and Blurred Painting

Among coloring methods, there is 'solid painting' in which color is applied evenly over the entire area, and 'blurred painting' in which it is blurred in areas away from the body. The blurred painting method is done with the light source in mind as shown below. Apply the color of the garment lightly on the side near the light source as the actual color in the center, and lighter again on the opposite side, while adding subtle shading at the end.

Solid painting

This method is effective when seeking a good contrast of shape and color. By accentuating lines or adding shading, you can create a three dimensional effect.

Blurred painting

This method can enhance the fabric texture and add depth to a drawing. It is less time consuming you color fewer areas using this method.

Coloring Steps

The following are the coloring steps. We use three types of tools. Gouache, markers, and color pencils. Do not try to color using a single stroke at first. Instead, use more strokes to improve the quality. Do not compromise when mixing color.

1. A sketch on copy paper. Minimize the creases.

2. Transfer sketch: Fill in reverse side with pencil and trace outline from front side.

3. As the transferred line is weak, complete it with pencil.

4. Set direction of the light, and apply skin color lightly. Make the shadow side a little darker.

5. Apply a lighter tone base color for the hair.

6. Color from the area you are sure of. Create the right color on the dish, and remove excess paint from the brush. As watercolor looks different when dry, do a trial run first.

7. Color starting from the underlayer and from large to small areas. Leave edges of upper layers (collar and belts) unpainted.

8. Rinse the brush lightly after every color application, and blur the areas away from the body.

9 . Complete details
   per item.

Add shading to the
scarf with marker.

Paint metallic parts
in gold or silver.

Create material
texture with color
pencil.

Review the
color scheme of
accessories.

Redraw erased lines.

Apply color to
accessories with pencil.

Add seams and
stitches, etc.

2 Patterns

Remember two key points when drawing patterns:

One is that, as the fabric surface changes, the pattern does also. As shown in illustrations 1, precise circle patterns appear as vertical ovals when the fabric is rolled or loosely folded. Another is that you should have paper patterns (illustration 2) of the garment in mind. This shows paper patterns on a checked fabric for cutting. Note the 'fabric grain' indicated by the red lines, which represent the vertical reference line of each part. Confirm the direction of fabric with the correct fabric grain based on the center front (C.F.), and draw so that the patterns appear natural.

1

2

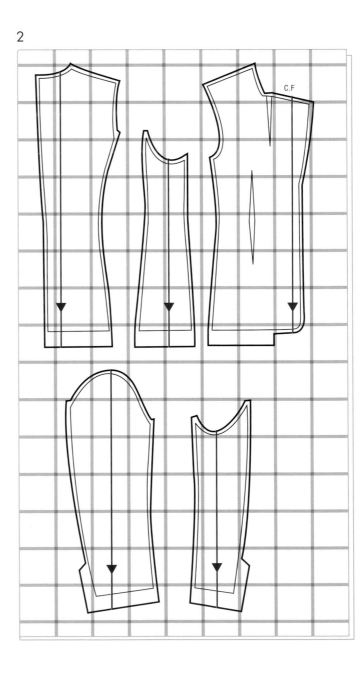

Not good   The fabric grains have not been considered. While the stripes on the skirt may look correct, when flattened, they appear unnatural.

Good   Patterns have been applied correctly, by considering the fabric grains of the jacket sides, sleeves, and the skirt.

Various Patterns

Patterns are created by printing and weaving, and come in many styles. Some representative ones are essential for you to practice. Draw patterns in the same order as if printing, i.e. from the bottom to top layer one by one. Markers and transparent watercolors are suitable for areas where colors overlap.

Pin Stripe	Pin Dot Stripe	Horizontal Stripe (fine)	Windowpane
Pencil Stripe	Hickory Stripe	Horizontal Stripe (medium)	Tattersall Stripe
Chalk Stripe	Thick & Thin Stripes	Horizontal Stripe (bold)	Gingham
Single Stripe	Multiple Stripes	Thick & Thin Horizontal Stripes	Tone-on-Tone Check
Double Thick & Thin Stripes	Sucker Stripe	Multiple Horizontal Stripe	Shepard's Check

Grain Check

Dots

Floral

Leopard skin

Houndstooth

Dots

Floral

Zebra skin

Argyle

Checkerboard

Floral (wall paper style)

Camouflage

Tartan

Optical (single color)

Nordic

Primitive

Tartan

Optical (multi-color)

Paisley

Herringbone

3 Materials

Material Rendition

Remember to always think of 'line in association with the coloring'. This is the key point regarding material rendition involving coloring. We normally adjust this balance as we draw without realizing it, but tend to overdraw when we are not familiar with the garment materials. No improvement can be expected if you limit the types of line without any particular reason or always use the same coloring method. Practice effective line rendition and coloring together, as the texture of the material is an important factor in fashion design drawing.

As shown below, you can depict the thickness or softness of the fabric texture on the same design drawings by varying the detail. Illustrations A and B on page 87 show these after coloring using the solid painting and blurred painting methods plus diagonal lines to represent the woven fabric texture.

Study that the balance of "lines and coloring" has an immediate influence on the fabric texture, by practicing coloring.

A Thin and sharp effect   **B** Slightly thicker and soft effect

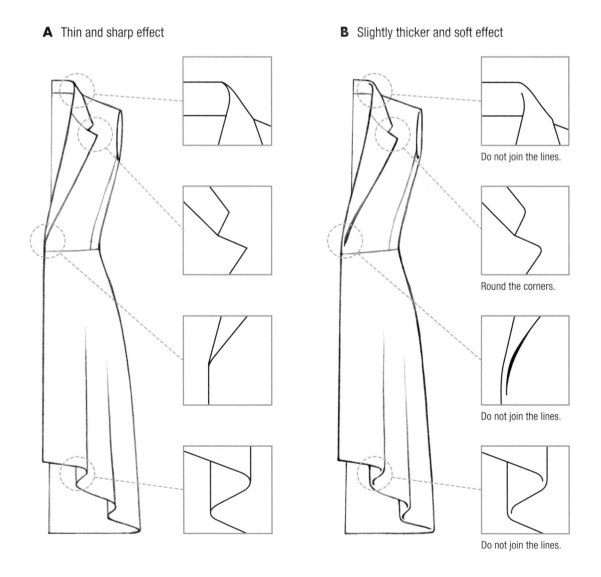

Do not join the lines.

Round the corners.

Do not join the lines.

Do not join the lines.

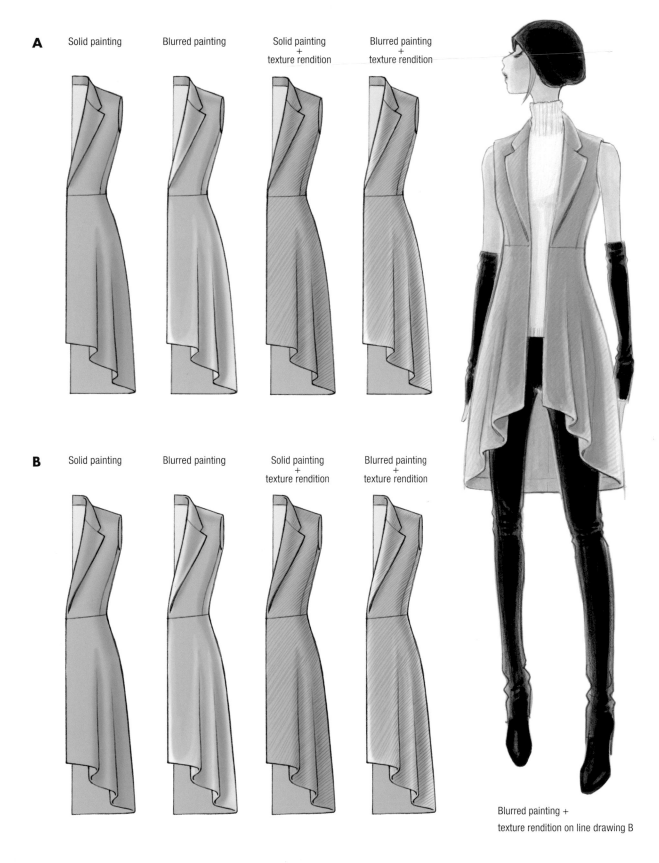

A
Solid painting Blurred painting Solid painting + texture rendition Blurred painting + texture rendition

B
Solid painting Blurred painting Solid painting + texture rendition Blurred painting + texture rendition

Blurred painting +
texture rendition on line drawing B

4 Drawings of Various Materials

Thin Materials/See-through Materials

Render thin materials in a thin line with a light touch, imagining them swaying in the breeze. Render see-through materials, keeping the following in mind regarding the transparency and overlapping of colors.

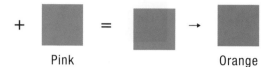

Yellow + Pink = Orange

As the above method creates a too transparent glass-like effect, adjust the transparency to create a fabric look.

Further, by adding contrasting density in overlapped areas and combining lines, you can distinguish the layers and show their relationship. (Lines of the underlayer should be broken towards the end.)

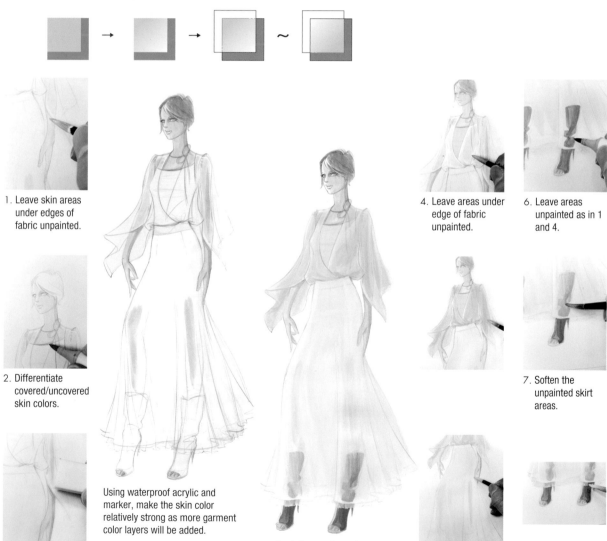

1. Leave skin areas under edges of fabric unpainted.

2. Differentiate covered/uncovered skin colors.

3. Erase lines under the fabric.

Using waterproof acrylic and marker, make the skin color relatively strong as more garment color layers will be added.

Apply base color, using watercolors and marker.

4. Leave areas under edge of fabric unpainted.

5. Add watercolor to skin, blurring the outline to show thinness of fabric.

6. Leave areas unpainted as in 1 and 4.

7. Soften the unpainted skirt areas.

8. Apply white to the hem lace.

9. Adjust hair/
   make-up to suit
   fabric colors with
   watercolor.

10. Color the details
    using watercolor.

11. Add pencil lines
    paying attention
    to the layers.

12. Draw lace
    patterns using
    pencil.

13. Accentuate key
    places with gray
    marker.

Adjust details and colors using
watercolor, marker and pencil.

Knit/Cut & Sewn

The key feature of knit, cut, and sewn fabrics is elasticity. They are not suitable for designs in which the fabrics have no contact with the body due to gravity. Note that darts and drapes are also difficult to produce with these fabrics for the same reason.

It is necessary to focus on the difference between low, medium, and high knitting gauges, versatile types, and the jointed parts of knit fabrics. In these, the creases and sagging appear in a layered ring-like spring form.

1. Use gray marker for creases at under bust, waist, and elbows.

2. Apply white watercolor to soften the creases.

3. Use gray marker for vertical drapes.

Add the major stitches at the line drawing stage.

Base coloring

4. Use gray marker for unevenness of knit surfaces.

5. Apply watercolor. Blur and leave edges unpainted.

6. Draw stitches with color pencil.

7. Draw lightly more stitches with pencil.

8. Adjust outline of the vest, adding unevenness.

9. Add mottled nubs with pencil.

10. Draw the ribs in delicate lines.

11. Draw stitches with color pencil.

Draw details.

12. Draw gathers with pencil.

13. Apply shading to drapes with gray marker.

14. Adjust the outline with pencil.

15. Highlight cable stitches with white watercolor.

16. Use gray marker to finish as necessary.

Cotton/Denim

The key features of cotton include that it easily acquires creases, which are difficult to remove, and that its alternating creases form various triangles. As the seams of cotton garments are often finished with top-stitches, be sure to draw them in a dotted line or finer line. To draw denim jeans successfully, pay attention to the unique surface texture, degree of faded indigo, and fine details around the hips. Practice while taking time and care.

Apply skin color with marker.

Apply base color with watercolors.

1. Leave crease ridgelines unpainted.

2. Use side of color pencil lead to draw texture and faded indigo-look.

Draw surface texture with color pencils.

Complete details with watercolors, markers, and pencil.

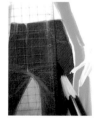

3. Draw faded indigo on twills/warps/stitches with color pencils at a slight angle.

4. Add stitches in a lighter green.

5. Add stitches strongly on denim.

6. Add shading as flat triangles with gray marker.

7. Color the rivets and buttons.

8. Give depth by shading to the sides with gray marker.

9. Redraw outlines, creases and details, with pencil.

10. Add highlights to metal parts to complete.

Autumn/Winter Materials [1]

In general, garment materials for autumn and winter should be drawn with a soft image to give a sense of warmth. Use soft lines especially for the outline and structural lines of woolen materials, while giving consideration to their thickness. Color the base using the blurred painting method, and complete while paying extra care to rendition of the fabric to enhance the vividness of your drawing.

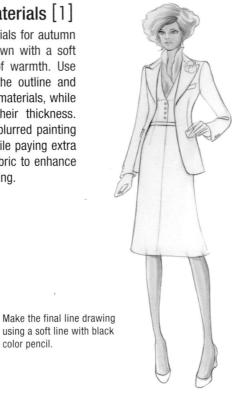

Make the final line drawing using a soft line with black color pencil.

1. Apply watercolors with a broad brush stroke. Disregard details such as lines.

2. Carefully blur edges with a brush using water and draw woven patterns with color pencil.

3. Add tweed nubs randomly with brown marker.

4. Add nubs on the outline, using brush tip with ivory watercolor.

5. Add herringbone with white watercolor using flat brush.

6. Draw lace on the collar with white watercolor.

Completion of the base coloring

Adjustment and completion of details

7. Add luster with white color pencil.

8. Adjust hair and make-up.

9. Add gray so that the skin color shows through.

10. Apply shading first with gray marker.

11. Add luster with white color pencil.

12. Color buttons with brown watercolor.

13. Color the corsage with ivory watercolor.

14. Add shading with gray marker.

15. Complete lines with black pencil.

Autumn/Winter Materials [2]

In addition to wool, there is a wide range of fabric materials such as quilting, corduroy, boucle, gabardine, and velour for autumn and winter. Practice drawing their texture by adding an extra touch to the outlines or surfaces to bring out their features.

Make the final line drawing using black color pencil. Draw thin keylines for quilting stitches on the cape.

1. Apply watercolor broadly. Leave some areas unpainted for loose fitting look.

2. Imagining the fabric texture, adjust blurring with watercolor.

3. Reduce the color tone with gray marker.

4. Leave quite a lot unpainted for a fluffy look.

Completion of the base coloring.

Add the fabric texture.

5. Color sunglasses and hair with watercolor.

6. Draw unevenness of the quilting using dark brown color pencil for the shadows.

7. Use white pencil for the lit area.

8. Alternate white pencil and gray marker to represent ribs.

9. Blur color of scarf in patches with watercolor.

10. Use tip of brush to draw the frizzy end.

11. Add gabardine twills on the outline using flat brush with white watercolor.

12. Add contrasting lines with the black pencil used for final line drawing.

13. Draw stitches carefully with color pencil/mechanical pen.

14. Draw an indent where the stitches meet the outline.

15. Make the corduroy outline uneven.

16. Add shading with gray marker to give volume.

Leather/Fur

Leather and fur come in a considerable number of types when including artificial ones. Roughly classified, leather consists of shiny and mat, and fur of those with long hair and short hair. As each has a unique appearance, it will be good training for you to draw them.

At the final line drawing stage, draw the hairs of fur and soft creases of leather.

1. Apply the base watercolor thinly. When half-dry, paint dark color over it.

2. Apply solid coloring with watercolor to smaller areas, i.e. leather.

3. Leave quite a lot of fur unpainted for a fluffy look.

4. Carefully blur the edges with brush and water.

5. Layer colors roughly to render the hairs of fur.

6. Apply watercolor to produce mottled effect on the suede.

Render the features of leather and fur at the base coloring stage.

7. Scrape white pastel and pick up on a blending stump.

8. Apply pastel to shiny ridgelines of creases. Erase excess pastel.

9. Go over the surface with black pencil.

10. Using brush tip, paint hairs on the leather beneath.

11. Add slightly different tone of fur color using brush tip.

12. Reduce color tone and draw hairs on the shadow side.

13. Add shine with white watercolor on ridgelines of creases.

14. Apply shading with gray marker on right of ridgelines.

15. Render the short haired boa with colored dots.

16. Blur the suede with white pencil.

17. Adjust fur by adding hairs with pencil.

18. Add a few more hairs with black pencil on shadow side.

19. Redraw hidden lines with black pencil.

20. Give a final touch to all lines with pencil.

Shiny Materials

If you draw shiny materials from the photographs of fashion magazines, you will find it very difficult as there are too many light sources. So when making a design drawing, set a more simple light source to minimize this problem. It also makes drawing easier if you classify materials by those with a single light source and those with an irregular reflection without a set light source. When setting a light source, it is recommended to cast the light along the 'ridgeline' starting from the shoulder to the center of the knee through the top of the breast.

At the line drawing stage, have in mind which areas to make shiny.

1. Blur color along the fabric drapes with watercolor.

2. Remove color from lit areas with water on a brush.

3. Be sure not to paint the lit areas.

At the base coloring stage, separate the areas for blurring and nonpainting. The blurred pink areas are those with an irregular reflection, and the unpainted blue areas have a set light source.

4. Adjust overall color of skirt, by applying reflected color.

5. Leave protruding areas unpainted.

Adjust the light and reflection.

6. Tap pink watercolor randomly on blurred areas.

7. Render irregular light reflections as white dots.

8. Add darker pink to increase contrast with dots.

9. Add slightly larger white dots to areas with most reflection.

10. Add shadows below unpainted areas with gray marker.

11. Add highlights as shown in 9.

12. Render metallic luster.

13. Adjust hair/ make-up with color pencil and watercolor.

14. Add highlights on accessories using white.

15. Add highlights as shown in 14.

16. Complete by adding shadows with gray marker.

5 Processing by Computer

Versatile Processing

Based on the fashion design drawing, the garment will be developed into a commercial item. A good color variation is essential as it could largely determine the success of its sales, even when the form and materials are the same. It is important to carry out sufficient color simulations before deciding on the final color selection. Mastering the process to produce color variations of the design drawing using the computer, you will discover new potentials for the garment, and also create smooth presentations. Here I introduce an example of the process using Photoshop with basic and minimum operation.

* Preparation: Scan your drawing by setting the output resolution to between 150dpi - 300dpi, and trimming the desired part in the preview mode.

1. **Correction**
Using the Levels dialog (1-2)" ('Image' > 'Adjustments' > 'Levels'), correct the sharpness of the scanned image (1-1), by moving the two triangles towards the center while observing the changes in the image window. Select the 'Layers' ('View' > 'Layers') and click 'Duplicate Layer' (1-4).

! Remember to save the data at every stage.

1-1 The scanned image

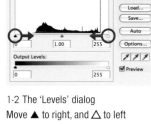

1-2 The 'Levels' dialog
Move ▲ to right, and △ to left

1-3 Sharp image after correction

1-4 Duplicate "Layer"

2. **Selecting a specific area**
Select the garment item on which you want change color. Choose the Magic Wand tool from the Tools-palette (2-1), and click the area where the color of the item is most stable. Until the flickering broken line (2-2) outlines the entire item, continue selection (2-4), by adjusting the Selection modes of the Magic Wand tool; 'Add to selection', 'Subtract from Selection', 'Tolerance' and 'Contiguous', etc. (2-3). Complete selection (2-7), by adding and deleting details with the Lasso tool (2-5, 6).

! You can undo each step by selecting 'Edit' > 'Undo'

2-1

2-2 Active flickering selection range

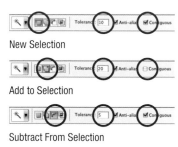

New Selection

Add to Selection

Subtract From Selection

2-3 Adjustment with Magic Wand Tool

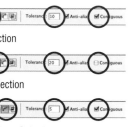

Add

Subtract

2-5 Adjustment by Lasso tool

2-4 Continue selection by changing clicking positions with Magic Wand tool

2-6 Fine-tuning by Lasso tool

2-7 Selection completed successfully

3. Modifying colors

When the garment item is outlined and selected perfectly, copy it ('Edit' > 'Copy') and paste it back into the image window ('Edit' > 'Paste'). Select the new Layer in the 'Layers' palette (3-1). Select the 'Hue/Saturation' dialog ('Image' > Adjustments > 'Hue/Saturation') (3-2), and modify the color by moving the sliders; Hue, Saturations, and Lightness (3-3, 3-4).

3-1 When pasted, it appears automatically·as a new layer.

3-2 Hue/Saturation dialog

3-3 Adjustment of the hue

3-4 Only the color of selected item is changed.

4. Creating variations

Per each garment item, select the 'Background' layer in the Layers palette and do select, copy, and paste. Repeat 'Duplicate Layer' in the 'Layers' palette, and adjustment by the "Hue/Saturation" (4-1, 2), and you can freely produce color variations. Once you are satisfied with the color simulations, enlarge the image by selecting "Canvas Size" from the "Image Menu", and you can make an effective presentation layout (4-3).

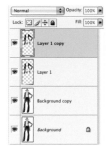

4-1 Repeat the 'Duplicate Layer'

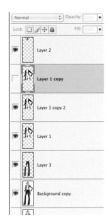

4-2 Repeat the process on hat and pants.

4-3 Making full use of the advantages of computer enables the simulation of various coordinations.

Lesson

4

Exercise by Garment Item

1 Technical Drawing

What is Technical Drawing?

Fashion design drawing alone cannot communicate the precise specifications of each garment item. A technical drawing of each item is essential in the process of apparel production. It depicts the item's structure in a simple line as shown below and color may be applied as required. Technical drawing aims to communicate the balance, structure, and specifications, and is usually accompanied by the back style of the garment.

Fashion design drawing

Technical drawings

F.S   B.S

Lengths and Divisions

Before drawing each garment item, confirm the names of the dividing lines on the upper wear and the length of the garment. Names such as 'high waist, natural waist, and low waist' often refer to the positions of the joining and tapering of the top wear and waist position of the bottom wear. The 'micro' and those below are the names for lengths of the skirt and coat. When making technical drawings, be sure to carefully set such a length and not to be caught up with other details only. Be sure that these positions are in good balance with the entire body.

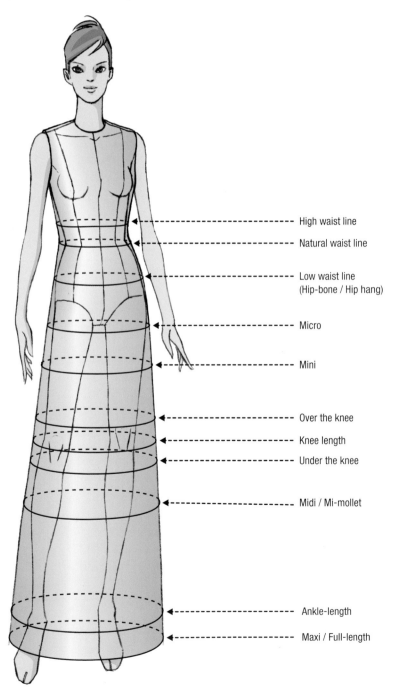

High waist line

Natural waist line

Low waist line
(Hip-bone / Hip hang)

Micro

Mini

Over the knee

Knee length

Under the knee

Midi / Mi-mollet

Ankle-length

Maxi / Full-length

Characteristics of Garment Item

In addition to the balance of length and line, structure and specifications, there is one more point that you must pay attention to when making technical drawings. It is to understand the characteristics of each item. The sleeve of the tailored jacket (illustration 1) is drawn in a very clean line and seems technically correct, but in fact it is wrong. When a sleeve is lifted this much, the armhole also lifts, creating many creases from the front button through the bust area (illustration 2). In order to present a tailored jacket in a simple and clean line while conveying its characteristics, illustration 3 is sufficient. On the other hand, in the case of drawings of sports and work wear which allow more movement space for the sleeves, large creases will appear from the under arm.

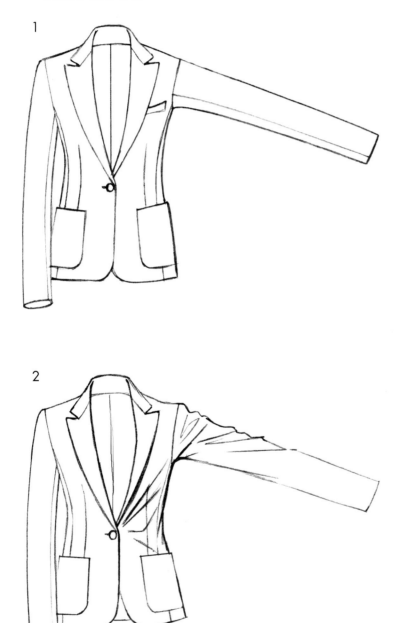

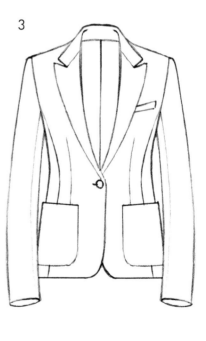

In some cases, both are not wrong (illustrations 4, 5, and 6), and you should select the drawing most suited for the purpose, i.e. for depicting the characteristics of the garment.

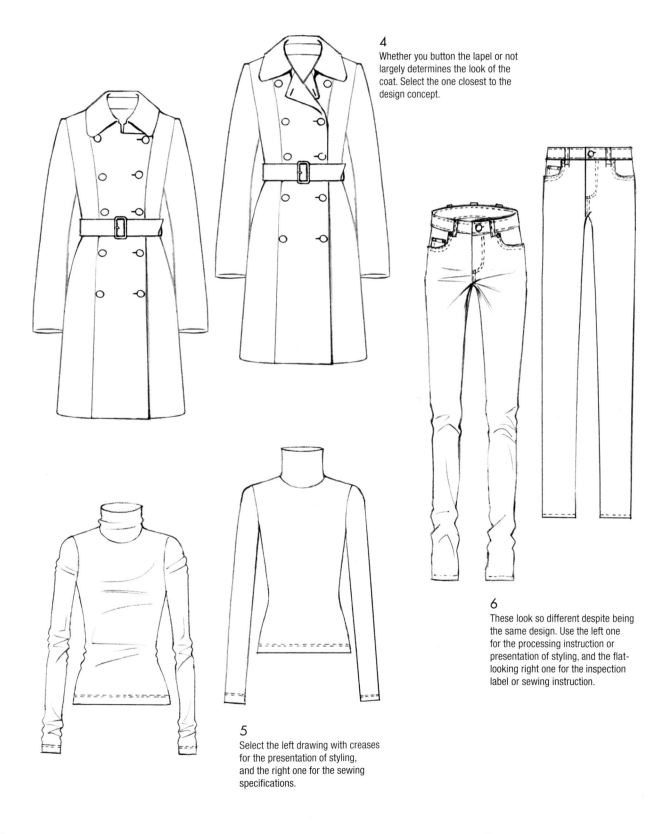

4
Whether you button the lapel or not largely determines the look of the coat. Select the one closest to the design concept.

6
These look so different despite being the same design. Use the left one for the processing instruction or presentation of styling, and the flat-looking right one for the inspection label or sewing instruction.

5
Select the left drawing with creases for the presentation of styling, and the right one for the sewing specifications.

Master Template

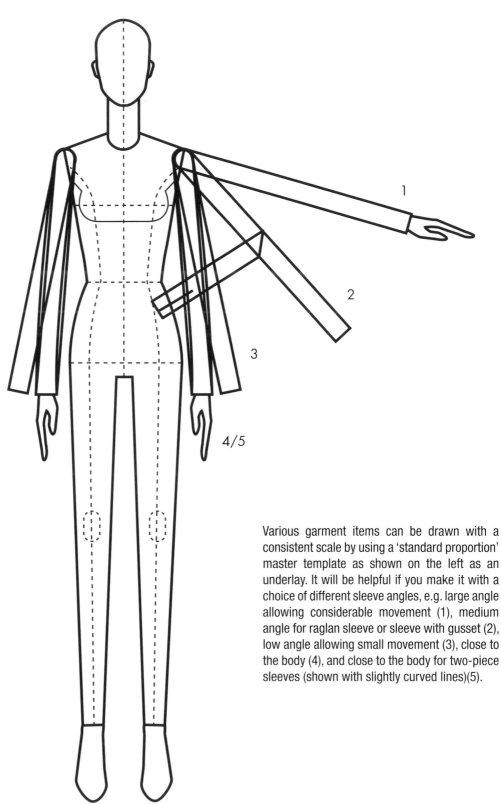

Various garment items can be drawn with a consistent scale by using a 'standard proportion' master template as shown on the left as an underlay. It will be helpful if you make it with a choice of different sleeve angles, e.g. large angle allowing considerable movement (1), medium angle for raglan sleeve or sleeve with gusset (2), low angle allowing small movement (3), close to the body (4), and close to the body for two-piece sleeves (shown with slightly curved lines)(5).

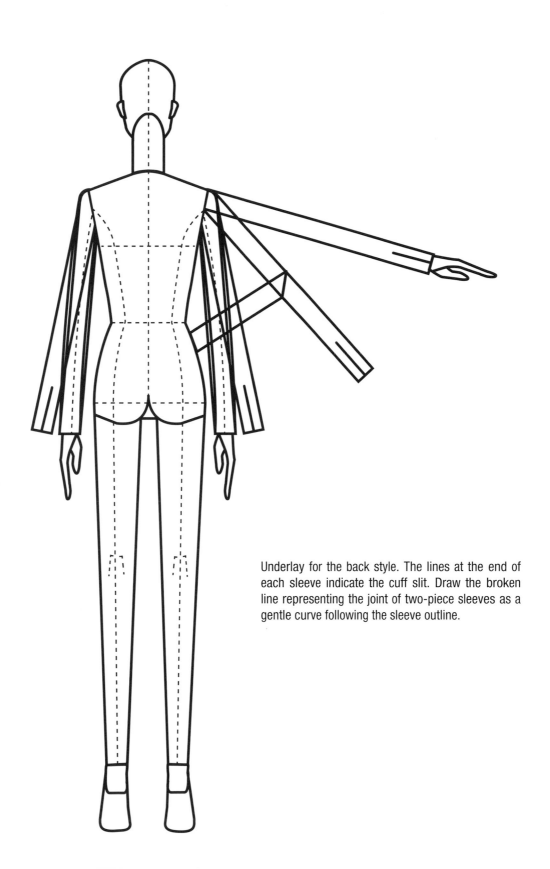

Underlay for the back style. The lines at the end of each sleeve indicate the cuff slit. Draw the broken line representing the joint of two-piece sleeves as a gentle curve following the sleeve outline.

2 Technical Drawing Steps

The following are the technical drawing steps when made by hand. Use a hard pencil, ruler, template, marker, and color pencil on copy paper.

1. Place a piece of copy paper on the master template.

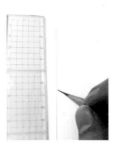

2. Draw the centerline with pencil.

3. Hold the pencil lightly and sketch the outline in a clean line.

4. Use a grid-ruler to check symmetry.

5. Complete positioning of parts and outlines based on overall balance.

6. Ink with fine drawing pen. Correct any errors later.

7. Use a ruler for straight lines, and template for buttons.

8. Erase pencil lines completely.

9. Apply solid painting in light fabric color with marker.

10. Apply a darker color with marker except at the edges.

11. Blur the dark color by going over the entire area with the light color marker used for 9.

Completion of base
coloring with marker

Completion of fabric texture
rendition with color pencil

12. Add ridgelines of
the weave with gray
color pencil.

13. Add shadows under
the raised areas.

14. Add highlights on
the button with
white watercolor or
correction pen.

15. Paint out any unwanted
lines or areas with
white watercolor or
correction pen.

Completion

3 Technical Drawings by Computer

Creating Parts

When making technical drawings manually, it is rather difficult to maintain symmetry or to draw stitches. You may also have to start all over again from the line drawing if a correction becomes necessary. Using the computer enables you to draw garment parts more quickly and precisely, and to make alterations and corrections very easily. Here I introduce such an example, using Adobe Illustrator.

1. Preparation

Scan a draft of the technical drawing to a computer, and open a new document ('File' > 'New Document'), and then place the scanned image ('File' > 'Place'). In the Layers palette ('Window' > 'Layers') check the 'Lock' option of the active layer (1-1), and add a new layer (1-2). Select the Pen tool in the Toolbox (1-3), and set the 'Stroke' to red to differentiate from the draft line (1-4).

1-1 Click the 'Lock' option.

1-2 New 'Layer'

1-3

1-4 Stroke: red; Fill: none

2. Creating parts

Using the Pen tool, draw each individual part separately, starting from an underlayer in the order of front body, sleeve, under collar, top collar, pockets, and button (2-1). Draw the right side of jacket only.

2-1 Use a different colored line for each part so that it is readily identifiable.

3. Making symmetry

Select all parts drawn as above, and do 'Copy' and 'Paste' (3-1). Display 'Reflect' ('Object' menu > 'Transform' > 'Reflect') and select 'Vertical' to reverse the parts (3-2). Move the reversed parts and place them symmetrically on the other side (3-3). Select 'Select All' from the 'Edit', and set the 'Stroke' to black and 'Fill' to white (3-4). Select a finer line to draw darts and other fine lines, click the eye icon on the Layers palette to make the draft invisible (3-5). While holding down the Shift key, continuously select the entire right front body and left collar with the Selection tool (Black Arrow) (3-6), and do 'Bring to Front' ('Object' > 'Arrange' > 'Bring to Front') (3-7).

3-1 Copy/Paste

3-2 Select 'Vertical'.

3-3 When moving more than one, select 'Group' from the 'Object' menu.

3-4 Stroke: black; Fill: white

3-5 Make the draft invisible.

3-6 Select the right front body and left collar only.

3-7 Completion of symmetry after 'Bring to Front'.

4. Alteration of parts

Using the Pen tool, set the dashed line: 1 pt for 'dash' and 2 pt for 'gap' (4-1) in the Stroke palette, and add stitches to the edges of the collar, front closure and pockets (4-2). Fill in each part with color. As an easy alteration, create a new layer for additional buttons. Using the Rectangle tool (4-3) and Pen tool, create a square-cornered pocket flap (4-4), and replace the original one (4-5). Copy and paste the collar, select the anchor points you want to move with the Direct Selection tool (White Arrow) (4-6), and complete alteration of the collar (4-7).

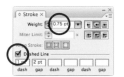

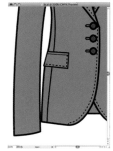

4-1 Enter 0.75 pt for 'Weight', check 'dashed line' box and set 'dash' and 'gap' values.

4-2 Neat stitches that are easy to control.

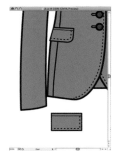

4-3

4-4 New part

4-5 Additional buttons and altered pocket.

4-6 Widen the lapel using the Direct Selection tool.

4-7 You will be able to quickly check changes if you create parts on each layer.

Converting Colors/Adding Patterns

Using Illustrator, you can change colors and add patterns very quickly. All you have to do to change colors is select the part and select a new color on 'Fill'. Create patterns before hand and save them in the Swatches palette as stock. Using a computer enables clean renditions as shown below, and dramatically expands your design potential.

4 Drawings of Various Items

*Examples of technical line drawings are shown per separate garment item group for reference.

Knitwear

Rib-knit sweater

Round-neck sweater

High-neck sweater

Buttoned cardigan

Cable-knit vest

Rib-knit cardigan with belt

Lace-knit sweater

Cut & Sewn

Cowl-neck shirt

Sweatshirt

Ruffled skirt

Cardigan

Hooded sweatshirt

Leggings

Polo shirt

Cache coeur

Skirts

Mini/hip-hung

Knee length/barrel

Below-knee length/
tight with slit

Below-knee length/
wraparound

Above-the-knee
length/box pleated

Mimolle length/flared

Ankle length/pleated

Mimolle length/gathered

Mimolle length/goared

Pants

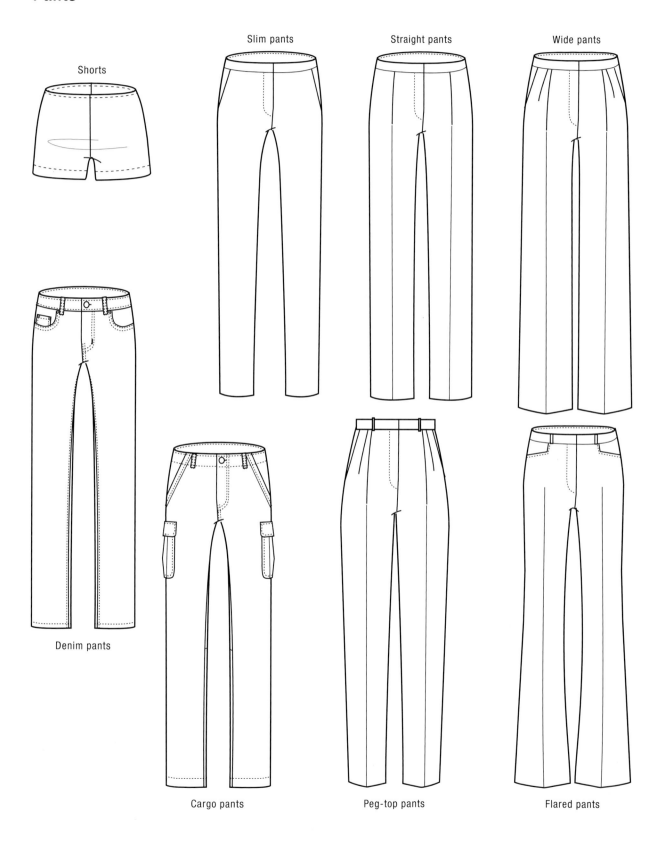

Shorts

Slim pants

Straight pants

Wide pants

Denim pants

Cargo pants

Peg-top pants

Flared pants

Tailored Jackets

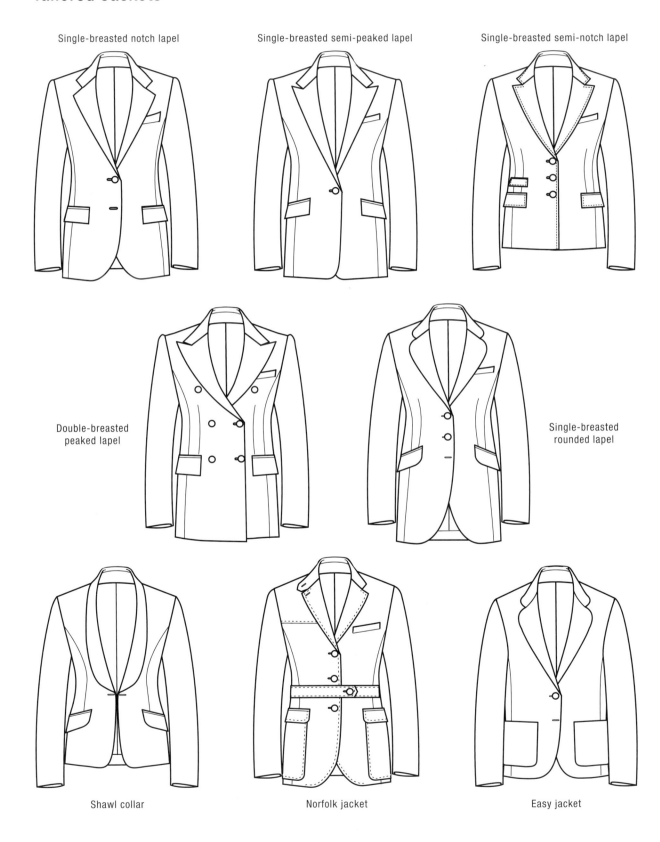

Single-breasted notch lapel

Single-breasted semi-peaked lapel

Single-breasted semi-notch lapel

Double-breasted
peaked lapel

Single-breasted
rounded lapel

Shawl collar

Norfolk jacket

Easy jacket

Jackets/Blousons

Cardigan jacket

Trim blazer

Pea coat

Windbreaker

Letter jacket

Riders jacket

Denim jacket

Coats

Trench coat

Duffle coat

Balmacaan coat

Wraparound coat

Underwear

Brassiere

Camisole

Corset

Slip

Tank top

Halter-neck

Garter belt

Babydoll

Panties

Stockings

Postscript

How well did you do?

I wanted this book consist of double-page spreads, each dealing with a single topic so that you could take a look and then, when you had grasped the idea, start drawing. If you got stuck during a piece, I wanted you to be able to flip back through the pages. You can use it as a textbook, methodically working your way from beginning to end, or as a reference book by focusing on a specific section.

When I encounter students who do not know what to draw or make, I provide them with a motivation to draw. They then begin sketching with the idea of creating something, and as time passes the sketchbook fills with a varied record of the things they have created. This accumulated record of encounters with one's own creativity constitutes a good warm-up practice for making fashion design drawings. The same inflection of a line, the same colors and shapes appear again and again, along with scribbled notes. When you begin to know the value of these, practice repeatedly to lay down the foundations, and keep sketching, your design drawings will begin to acquire individuality and quality. These are characteristics common to people already active in the apparel design world. In practice, design drawings are almost always completed in one go. That is because you are trying to get the idea buzzing in your head down before it flies away. If you are having trouble expressing something while you draw, try copying the techniques described in this book. No matter how much copying you do, the record that stays in your sketchbook will be your own. You can never make a perfect copy, and that's what makes drawing and design so interesting.

For me this book is a labor of gratitude. If it had not been for the encouraging words and cooperation of people who supported me, I would never have completed it, and I have had my muse restored numerous times by the great pictorial work and research left behind by our predecessors in the collections of drawings and reference books on my bookshelf. To name a few: Junko Yamamoto of the Kuwasawa Design School, who inspired me to create this book; Masataka Ohno and Kinji Watanabe of Daimaru Graphics, who gave me useful advice from when I first started writing it; the designers Noboru Okano and Megumi Ohiyama, who provided wonderful designs despite their extremely busy schedule; Miki Kobayashi of swanky, who generously provided model photographs; Sotaro Hirose, who took the photographs of the artist's materials; and of course Sachiko Oba of Graphic-sha Publishing Co. Ltd., who gave me encouragement on numerous occasions during my several months of slow progress and somehow managed to guide me through to completion. I take this opportunity to express my greatest thanks to them all.

Lastly, to all the readers who take this book in hand, my sincere thanks. I will be happy if it helps you find wings for your own expression and to take flight into the world of fashion design.

About the Author

Naoki Watanabe

1963   Born in Tokyo

1984   Graduated from the KUWASAWA DESIGN SCHOOL (Dress Design Department)
        Studied under Reiko Saito
        Entered Setsu Mode Seminar

1987   Instructor at the KUWASAWA DESIGN SCHOOL and Oda Fashion College in Tokyo